Rebecca Blum

***

Inside The War Room

Copyright © 2019 Rebecca Blum

Publisher: tredition GmbH, Halenreie 40-44, 22359 Hamburg, Germany
Cover Design: Rebecca Blum

ISBN
Paperback: 978-3-7497-5660-5
Hardcover: 978-3-7497-5661-2
eBook: 978-3-7497-5662-9

Printed on demand in many countries

Table of Contents

Preface

They say love is a battlefield. I think all human relations are a battlefield. And that, to be honest, means that life is a battlefield.

As a student of political science and geopolitics and, more recently, as a strategy consultant for the German Ministry of Defence, reading the works of military theorist Carl von Clausewitz is one of my favourite pastimes. Strategy excites me like nothing else about my work, and war and human relations are two equally intriguing arenas to employ strategy in. I like Clausewitz's take on the military and war a great deal because he has a unique way to factor in the *psychology* of actors and the peculiarities of politics. A theory of his that I find particularly interesting is 'the trinity'[i]. This concept explores how different forces, three to be exact, drive the trajectory of a battle. Clausewitz advises military actors to view their battles through the prism of his proposed trinity and to devise their strategies with the purpose of balancing its three forces.

I don't want to bore anyone with war theory, but Clausewitz's thoughts really resonate with me, and I find that his trinity is incredibly applicable to my understanding of interpersonal relations. So let me just give you a quick introduction.

The trinity consists of the following three realms: first, the blind force of passion or the inherent (psychological) dispositions of the parties that partake in a battle. Second, there is the way that creative genius and skill interact with chance and probability to execute a chosen strategy. Third, the larger (political) context and reason that dominates even the most perfected skills and the wittiest of strategies. In the original application of 'the trinity', that is in war, the first realm concerns the people. The second realm concerns the commander and his army, and the third realm concerns the government. In my application of the theory, for interpersonal relationships, the trinity concerns the different influences on our actions that are manifested in each of us and that affect our thoughts and decision making. The three realms are deeply rooted in all of us but can vary in their relationship with one another. We can look at all of them distinctly, but together, they make up each of our individual characteristic wholeness. Every decision we make may have a dominant influence from one of the realms – inherent passions and values, skill and chance or reason and context – but they will never be completely separate from the other elements in the other realms. For example, we can make decisions that are based solely on our skillset, and the odds may be in our favour so that the use of our skills makes us successful in completing a task. But our decision to make use of our skills will undeniably include considerations from past experiences, our values, our understanding of the context we find ourselves in and so forth.

In that way, the three realms can be thought of as our *why*, our *how* and our *what* in decision making. Getting to know ourselves at the deepest level and understanding the three realms for our individual case allows us to predict, understand, respect, appreciate and cherish ourselves and our actions.

Of course, the expression of our three realms interacts with and affects other actors' expression of their expressions of their realms. Our actions permeate each other's environments and contexts, making human interaction incredibly complex and complicated. The more we aim to align our realms with those of other people, the more complex and complicated it becomes and the more energy it takes for this combination of two or more peoples' realms to first occur and then be successful. It can be pretty easy to share a worldview with someone else and make circumstantial decisions together based on this worldview. But it requires a lot more effort to share a worldview, have the same understanding of what actions are 'the right' ones based on this worldview and also share our inherent values that inform this understanding with another person.

Passions. People. Context.

Values. Experiences. Skills. Circumstance.

So many things come together as we try to navigate our day-to-day battles of human interaction – our day-to-day battles of life. Looking at this subject, we'll go on to talk about innate preferences, inherent behaviours and habits, mental models, becoming aware of them through introspection, consciously acting on them or against them by taking responsibility and constantly outgrowing ourselves and replenishing our personal resources by committing to and respecting ourselves.

This book is a collection of reflections on interpersonal effectiveness that I put together as the story of my 'becoming'. It's at once a memoir, a meditation and a treatise. It's an exploration of my progress and growth, and I want to share the way in which I built a mental culture around self-awareness, a sense of agency, self-regulation, self-motivation and social awareness, at the core of which lies a profound sense of belonging and serving something larger than the self. This exploration takes place through my take on seven actions – or battles – that

I view as paramount in human interaction: asking, giving, taking, sharing, receiving, refusing and imagining.

In the battle of asking, we'll discuss forming a relationship with ourselves and looking for our own self-worth and identity in ourselves to unlock our inner resources. We'll talk about respecting ourselves, knowing ourselves deeply and accepting those deepest parts of our self before being able to enter into relationships that are sustainable. We'll then go on to discussing expectations and investments in relationships in the battle of giving. I'll lead into the idea of what and how much we should give, dealing with deficiencies in our relationships and knowing what to give, when to give it - and when we can't or shouldn't give. In the battle of taking we'll discuss basic human needs, individual priorities and how to deal with conflicts that arise based on them. We'll talk about values that are attached to our needs and decipher the mental code that drives each of our behaviour. In the battle of sharing, we'll go on to explore the positive effects of opening up to other people and resonating with their reactions to us. We'll discuss how being open to challenge will strengthen our resilience and emotional groundedness and how we should all develop the courage to share ourselves with others to question potentially harmful mindsets we hold on to and flourish optimally. In the battle of receiving, I'll lead into the concept of attachment styles. We'll discuss how our upbringing and early parental care influence our relationships, motivation and goal setting later in life. By understanding how we're wired based on this, we'll discuss setting meaningful goals and being driven to realise our ambitions by finding the reasons why we commit to things. Going from setting meaningful goals to making better, more meaningful choices, we'll discuss healthy boundaries and the benefits of rejection in the battle of refusing. In the final chapter, the battle of imagining, we'll discuss tapping into our inner resources and cashing in on the edifice built by conquering the previous six battles. We'll talk about using the imagination to open up new possibilities and harness our full potential.

So you are now welcomed into my personal war room, my metaphorical place of tactical and operational art, where I strategise and process and analyse and retreat from the everyday battles of the interpersonal.

Introduction

Around this time last year, my boyfriend of one and a half years broke up with me. The reasons for his decision had nothing to do with me or our love, really. It was more something along the lines of him needing to find his way back to himself and sorting his life out before he could properly commit to someone in a long-term relationship. One and a half years aren't that long in the grand scheme, but that breakup really through me for a loop. We had been through quite some messed up stuff together.

When we met, he was not in a good place career-wise and, hence, financially. This resulted in many dependencies and relationships that weighed on him and caused him to feel an overall fatigue or desperation about how the labour market treated him, about how the educational system didn't easily grant him access to better opportunities and how the political system of his home country caused a lot of damage to him and his life. The work he found to finance at least the basic practicalities of life was characterised by, in my opinion, inhumane working hours and hard physical labour. As a result, his social life was not exactly flourishing. Overall, he had had it tough and was lonely over the years. Imagine all the baggage he brought into our relationship.

Two weeks into our being together, something life-changing happened to him, and it was heavy, both on him and on our relationship. Our little romantic bud was fragile at that point; I didn't know whether it would ever come to blossom – the odds were that we'd spend a few weeks together and then realise this whole thing could never work out.

Spoiler alert: things turned out very differently. Our feelings for one another became very deep and genuine; I had never experienced something like it before. I had never seen someone whose sole experience in life was to be abandoned and let down still had so much love to give. Maybe that's what made me love him so deeply – and what made the breakup so hard for me. That's my pathetic attempt to distil some words from all the layers of passion, intimacy and love there were between us – just to say that yes, one and a half years is not a long time, but I was at an incredible loss when he left me. After all, it's not the length of time we know someone that makes them special to us. It's what they brought into our lives.

Anyway, what I set out to say here is not about him – it's about me. It's about a journey that I embarked on; it's about my growth and what I learned about myself and for myself that I want to share here.

***

I was scheduled to take a short business trip to Brussels about a week after we broke up. I actually felt surprisingly ok. I ate more or less, I slept normally, I laughed, and I kept myself busy. I have a great support system, both within myself and from the people around me – we'll get to that more later.

I felt no resentment towards him, and I began to see the rational sides about his decision to end it. At that point, I was even glad that he made a decision after such a long time of going back and forth between 'yes, we can make this work' and 'no, I need to be alone'. I started seeing that he did need to work some things out before any relationship of his could properly function. Maybe I was getting it completely wrong, but as far as I could tell, he was in a dark place all throughout our relationship and was not emotionally available to cater to what a relationship needs. I think I was able to shed a little light on his darkness, and that's why for the good part of those twenty months or so, the relationship seemed to work just fine for the both of us. But after all the conversations we had, I understood his decision.

Despite all that, I have no words to describe the pain and the sheer magnitude of devastation I felt over the fact that I lost him as my life partner.

I had so many questions.

Was there anything I could have done to prevent this from happening? Was there anything I could do now to salvage what was broken?

What did he think he'd gain out of this? Could he explain to me what the reasons for his decision were?

Did he have an idea plan for how he'd go on from here?

How did he see this break up? Was it a necessary step that he simply needed to take, and did he still hope for something to happen between us in the future?

As I was on the plane home from my business trip in Brussels, I listened to a podcast[ii] that I follow regularly. The podcast is hosted by a life coach of some sort who touches on all different kinds of subjects with all different kinds of people to speak about their success stories, life lessons and advice they want to share. In this particular episode, the host was talking to a couples therapist who shared her views on 'the good relationship' and what it means to be faithful in a world where romance is run by the 'swiping culture'.

To be honest, the content of the podcast itself wasn't revolutionary. But man how her words triggered a revolution inside my brain – a beautiful unravelling inside of me. As I sat there, strapped into my seat on the plane with the lights of Berlin appearing as a sparkle against the night sky some 800 feet below me, I felt as though I had reached the epitome of enlightenment on what it means to love, to be loved, to commit, to accept, to respect – and to surrender.

The Battle of Asking or
Becoming our Most Resourceful Self

Make no mistake, these insights didn't drop on me over the duration of a continental flight. The groundworks were years in the making. I'll include all of that later. For now, let's start with the fundamentals: Why did I reminisce so much about my ex-boyfriend and how I made peace with his decision to leave me? Didn't I say I was going to talk about me? **My** journey? **My** growth? Well, yes. But here's the thing: the quality of our relationships – of any kind, either with family, friends, or partners – defines the quality of our life. And vice versa. As a result, if we're not happy in our intimate relationships, it's hard to find sustainable happiness in the other parts of our lives. At the same time, if we're not happy *without* our intimate relationships, we can never have happy intimate relationships. Cool, huh? So all we must do to reach eternal bliss is to be happy when we're alone…happy when we're not alone…and happy when being on our own while not being alone.

Let's unpack this. What is it that we assign to the term 'relationship'? What attributes define what we call a romantic partnership? Love. Sexuality. Passion, compassion. Understanding. Support. Intimacy. Friendship. Home. Family. Knowing someone to their core. Going beyond what the rest of the world knows about and shares with our partner. A unique and in-depth connection with someone that is translated into sharing one's hopes, dreams, fears, bodies, emotions, possessions and futures.

What this means is that we are asking our partner to provide us with what entire social structures once used to provide[iii]. What people once found in their tribe, their village, their community is what a single person is now expected to provide to us in a faithful, monogamous and loving tandem. In fact, not only do we expect our partners to provide us with compassion, reassurance, a financial partnership, sexual and emotional fulfilment and everything else that is supposed to come with a relationship, but we *rely* on them for those emotional and physical resources.

And here's the crux of the matter: Is it any wonder that in asking of our partners the provision of our entire wholeness, we end up seeking identity and self-worth in our relationships, ergo in others, instead of in ourselves? Not only is it unsustainable over the long run, robs us of our entire independence and sets us and our relationships up for failure, but it is also inherently destructive to the very identity we're trying to build. Think about it: the closer you become to the person you love and the more you merge your characters and personalities, habits and behaviours into one, the less you remain the person your partner once fell in love with. Your identity is consumed by your romantic relationship in a process that only started because you were trying to build your own identity in the first place – by looking for it in your significant other.

I'm not saying we should all live polyamorously and have several intimate romantic relationships with many partners at the same time to be able to claim different resources from each one and hence avoid being consumed all at once by just one person. I'm saying we have to stop searching for ourselves in someone else altogether. I'm saying we have to make choices about what is fair to ask of our partner and what is our own job to provide for ourselves. Both require investments, and we have to empower ourselves to make conscious decisions about the areas in which we invest in our partners and in what areas we should invest in ourselves and our personal networks.

I don't want to delve too deep into investing in our partners in this chapter; there will be more on that later on. For now, suffice to say that I want us to understand one thing: whatever it is that we ask of our partners, whatever it is that we yearn for, it needs to be cultivated. And continuously so. Neither fulfilment nor bliss nor love are constant states of enthusiasm; they arise from actions and behaviours that need to be fed with a permanent sense of resilience and a continuous pattern of devotion[iv]. It's hard work, but there is no way to avoid it.

Whether we talk about investing in ourselves or investing in our partners, we are talking about one common denominator: we need resources. Whatever we don't ask of our partners, we have to provide in some other way. Whatever we want to give to someone has to be provided to us first. So how do we grow into our most resourceful selves? My answer is we need to take responsibility for ourselves and what we do. I am convinced that an important key to living a life close to yourself and at peace with yourself comes from taking responsibility for everything that happens to you. It is empowering. There is power in responsibility. Responsibility is the ability to respond and to deal with your environment with anything that happens to you. Response-ability, if you will.

I will take a little detour through my personal development to explain how I came to this conclusion. As a child, I was not very popular in school. I was bullied for being overweight, I was being bullied for being a smart-ass and getting good grades, I sucked at playing sports and so on and so forth. I remember one morning in fourth grade when I was nine years old. I arrived at school for first period and found my classmates drawing a caricature of me on the board: a balloon with arms and a Hagrid-like mop of hair on its head. When they saw me come into the classroom, they quickly scattered, giggling and feeling great about themselves. I swallowed my tears, kept my head down and went to sit down in my chair. Incidents like this happened on a daily basis. My mum had some financial trouble after she divorced my father, so I never really had all the cool clothes from the hot brands; I never had lots of pocket money to spend on going to the movies or Starbucks with the rest of the cool kids. When I brought classmates over to my place for school group work, we weren't greeted by a plate of fruits that my mum had freshly chopped up after her morning yoga class and afternoon shopping trips with her girlfriends. No, my mum worked full time, and I had to learn to care for myself early on. In short, I couldn't provide anything to the kids in my class that would add to their popularity or prestige. I couldn't offer them anything they considered worthy of a friendship, let alone their respect.

Many nights before bed, my mum would sit by my side, and as she went to tuck me in, I cried about the fact that I didn't have friends, how the kids in my class didn't like me. In fact, they treated me like crap, and I never felt like I belonged to where I was. My mum's only response was that it's better to not have any friends than to have fake friends or to change who I am for anyone. Of course, as a desperate 11-year-old girl, not having friends was not really an option. Coming to terms with being bullied and being an outsider was not something I could settle for, and thus, I couldn't accept who I was without the approval of those kids I so desperately wanted to be friends with. So I remained unhappy with who I was and how I looked. I couldn't appreciate my own academic successes because I didn't have athletic successes as well; I couldn't appreciate the kids who did like me and shared my destiny as outsiders. Anyway, my teenage unhappiness is well documented on the many melodramatic pages of my diary, but that's not what I want to dwell on here.

My feeling of self-worth and self-confidence started to build when I was about 15. At the time, I met a girl, Danielle, who I got along with really well. Though we weren't close friends initially, we had a few conversations every now and then and sometimes hung out during school breaks. Danielle was one of those people who found a way to make it cool to be a nerd and who made it respectable to like everyone, no matter how unpopular that person was. I think she picked up on me not having a lot of self-worth and confidence. One day, she told me about a book she had read that touched on some of C.G. Jung's psychological ideas, especially the notion of the 'shadow-self'. She told me she loved the book, and she took so much from it. So she recommended I should read it too. To this day, I am grateful to her for lending me C.G. Jung's book.

In his book[v], Jung introduces the shadow is a metaphor to describe those aspects of our own personality that are hard to accept. It could be being greedy, manipulative or arrogant. The shadow is the opposite of what Jung calls the 'persona', the ideal version of ourselves that we appreciate and that embodies the way we'd like to see ourselves. Reading this book, I realised that even though I didn't have what I thought was necessary to make friends with, I should have been able to make friends without money, fancy clothes and an overbearing mother. Sure, the kids were cruel – all kids are. They made fun of me and bullied me, but I started to realise that I indeed had some really annoying sides to myself, like being a know-it-all and a goody two-shoes, snitching on the other kids when they were naughty. Danielle's book taught me how to thoroughly introspect and uncover parts of myself – my shadows, in C.G.

Jung's terms – that made up my inner reality and were just as much a reason for not being popular as not owning Abercrombie hoodies and UGG boots.

Working to accept our shadow – that is, to accept our whole – makes us a whole lot more authentic and self-confident. Accepting our shadow quite simply allows us to make peace with ourselves and our own limitedness. Two things come with accepting our shadow: relief and responsibility. First, there is relief because we are no longer at war with parts of ourselves; we are no longer under the pressure of having to hide parts of ourselves because we are incapable of facing our imperfections and limitations. Then, there is responsibility because we can no longer make excuses for our own predicaments; we have to own every single thing we say, we do, we don't do, we fail at or we excel at. I am convinced that making yourself defenceless to this level, to fully accept all of your shadows, is the greatest form of power and security we can cultivate. Only when you grow this close to yourself will you be able to catch yourself from wherever you fall, to hold your own hand through tough times and be your most shielded place of refuge within your own mind. You grow to become response-able – and that is extremely empowering.

Another important thing I have come to understand from reading Danielle's book is that no matter how much glamorous, prestigious or simply enjoyable company we keep, our inner self will remain present, whether we want it or not. We will continue to have to deal with who we really are, with that person living inside of us who produces our thoughts and harbours our emotions. I guess that if I hadn't had these tough times to deal with in high school, I never would have received the gift of this realisation. On the contrary – I'm actually more and more convinced that growing up in an environment that hands everything to you without struggle and never challenges you to outgrow yourself through experiencing failures, rejections or hardship gives rise to the tendency of expecting everything to originate from the outside – even the development and maturing of our inner self. Without ever having fallen, it's quite hard to experience and explore your own depth. At best, an environment that never forces us to deal with resistance can encourage us to find ourselves, but it will never challenge us to truly create ourselves and take responsibility for ourselves. External reality cannot provide inner growth. External realities are certainly what trigger inner growth. But that process isn't possible without self-nourishment, which must come from the inside.

For self-nourishment, in turn, to be successful, we each have to enter into a relationship with our self. We have to fall in love with our self, respect our self, be loyal to our self and know our self to the core - become established in the seat of self[vi], if you will. This has probably been my single most important life lesson so far: you are the only person who will definitely be with you until you die. You are the only person you will inevitably have to live with forever. Not the cool kids from school, not the stay-at-home, yoga-class-going socialite mums with their rich banker husbands and Ralph Lauren shirts. You.

Of course, the idea that you're the only person you'll inevitably have to live with forever and thus matters most is easier said than understood, much less cultivated and practised. I think a big hurdle that needs to be overcome is taking on our eternal duty of – here we go again – individual responsibility. Being respected and popular in any conglomerate of individuals, be it our clique at school, our workplace or society in general, gives us security. We reach this respected, popular position because we fit in. We are popular because we show the traits and behaviours and possess the skills that abide by the social benchmark. What *everyone* believes must, of course, be true. What *everyone* wants must be necessary to have and worth striving for. Otherwise, why would they *all* pursue it?

Gently and painlessly, we slip into the happy-go-luckiness of not having to take responsibility for anything, much like it used to be when we were still little kids and our mums and dads decided everything for us – and also bore the consequences for us.

With the prospect of such blitheness, why would we even begin to question the motives and decisions made by the alpha members of society and the groups we are part of? Though, when we experience exclusion and rejection or our successes fail to materialise in terms of social esteem, prestige and reputation, even though we carefully followed every social rule the popular successful people live by, we have no other choice but to internalise the understanding that our external circumstances cannot compensate for our internal reality.

Let that sink in here for a second. I'll repeat it: Our external circumstances – cannot compensate - for our internal reality.

If we're not happy with ourselves – for whatever reason – no external circumstance, be it popularity, success, wealth or beauty, will ever sustainably make us so. It probably wasn't **our** behaviour (i.e., internal reality) that got us popularity, success, wealth and beauty in the first place. We might have never been earnestly convinced about why we should live our life like everyone we see on Instagram (i.e., external circumstance). How can we cultivate an inner reality of happiness when it's built on all external stimuli, on prechewed and predigested truths served to us by those popular, respected members of a social group we strive to be? We can't. That's right. We can't because we can't take responsibility for something that we don't earnestly stand for, are truly committed to and honestly convinced of.

***

I assume that most people who have had to struggle to find their place, make peace with themselves and build their self-confidence, because they didn't just wake up like this endured at least a phase of self-loathing. It is only natural that we'd take insults, failures and exclusion very personally if we experience it continuously. If you constantly receive the feedback that something about you is not accepted by the opinion-making, taste-defining majority of people and the way you go about your life fails to make you well liked, successful and popular, no wonder you eventually start hating who you are and wishing you could be someone else. As a kid, whenever I made a wish while blowing out the candles on the birthday cake or when seeing a shooting star or when throwing a coin in a fountain, I'd always pray for waking up tomorrow and looking as pretty as that actress from that movie or being as popular as this girl in my class or magically having lots of money so I could pay for liposuction – no kidding, that's as bad as it was.

I remember feeling absolutely helpless in the face of all the changes I thought I'd have to make so that I could be who I wanted to be: pretty, popular and cool. I thought my problem of being popular and cool would be solved by being pretty. I felt that my social acceptance, as well as my self-acceptance, depended solely on being perceived as pretty, which in turn depended entirely on me losing a hefty amount of weight. But I was desperate and convinced I could never achieve the weight loss that'd be needed to look pretty. Well, waiting for your external reality to change or taking action to change the outside factors determining your inner reality doesn't solve your problems, at least not in the long term. By no means does this mean you should sit tight and do nothing – on the contrary, what will solve your problems in a sustainable way is a kind of action that demands a much greater effort than buying new clothes, going to the gym, excelling at your job and making lots of money, dating a beau or driving the new E Class. Or liposuction, for that matter. We need to introspect and tend to our inner reality to really explore the root of why we feel and think about ourselves the way we do. Taking external action can be extremely healing – but only after introspection. First, we need to develop a mechanism to find out what the right action for us will be on the outside so that we can make the inside feel better.

I hope that at this point, the importance of why we need to get to know ourselves so well and why it's imperative we explore our whole, including the shadows we talked about before, is becoming clear. You guessed it: It's all about response-ability. If we get to know ourselves, we'll be able to take responsibility for our state of mind and become one hundred percent capable of responding to our needs.

I find it somewhat ironic, if not tragic, that the only real access we have to our inside selves is through external circumstances. We identify with the conscious knowledge we have about ourselves. Unfortunately, though, science hasn't just yet gotten us far enough to tap into our subconscious and make use of those invaluable depths that store so much of what makes us who we are. As a result, we can only know ourselves in so far as we are mirrored by our surroundings. We orient ourselves mainly by observing and exploring our environment – our external circumstances – and we develop lots of witty techniques to adapt our physical and psychological resources to our environment. Think about what we talked about before: we are popular and successful mostly when we fit in and stick to the social norms and rules. Remember, what *everyone* believes must be true, right? And what *everyone* wants must be necessary to have and worth striving for, right? Because otherwise, why would *they* all pursue it?

The fulfilment of this task, of mirroring and adapting to our environment, mostly proves to be quite advantageous, and I guess more often than not, it successfully helps people navigate through their life – so much so that we don't question why we do things, whether we should be doing things a particular way or what the alternatives could look like. My good friend C. G. Jung would warn us, though, that if we keep living our lives like sheep, we end up putting our perception of our self as mirrored by society and measured by our level of popularity, beauty-standard-accordance, Instagram followers or bank-account-overflowingness – in place of our real being. Ok, ok, so C. G. Jung wouldn't know what the hell an Instagram is, but you get the point: by not questioning our motives and not consciously acting with purpose, we start slipping into a purely artificial world, one defined by the concepts that are highly valued by the social mainstream – even though we never asked ourselves whether we *should* highly value them for cultivating our inner reality.

I really don't know who the hell this trendsetter was, who taught us to be pretty, be popular, get rich or die trying. Man, I wish C. G. Jung had been a trendsetter. Or Buddha. Someone who would have taught everyone that if you're willing to make the effort of rigorous and continuous introspection and self-examination, you can uncover really important truths about yourself and deem yourself worthy of serious attention and sympathetic interest. You can, then, simply grow to be your most resourceful self.

I met a man in Thailand, a sort of Buddha disciple, who provided me with invaluable insights on this matter. He taught me about a Buddhist principle that feeds a mindset of viewing everything as a learning experience and embracing everything that happens to you as a part of your life. I was in Thailand on vacation, and naturally, I went to see a lot of temples and monasteries. I had seen many holy sites from all sorts of different religions before going to Thailand. I was able to see Hindu temples in India and Nepal, Muslim mosques all around the Middle East and, of course, Christian churches, cathedrals and chapels. None of them, however, were quite as serene as the Buddhist monasteries I visited.

Seated on the floor of one of these Thai monasteries and wrapped in his saffron robe was one of the monks living in the monastery. He had an almost childish smile (most of his teeth were missing) that transported a sort of ease and blitheness, maybe even a bit of blissful ignorance to everything that was going on in the world outside the monastery walls. Passing him, I smiled at him and I guess I performed a little awkward bow, thinking that such a divine religious person deserved some humility from a tourist invading his home. He smiled back at me and, with a gesture, invited me to sit next to him and rest for a minute in the shadow of the fig tree he was leaning against.

His English wasn't very good, but we exchanged a few words, introduced ourselves and made fun of an American lady who was clearly suffering from the humidity and searing heat. 'Look her, so funny', he said in his broken English, his toothless grin spreading from one ear to the other. I told him I admired the way he seemed to take on life with such ease and how he radiated joy, even though he must be so annoyed at all these white folks treating his home like a museum. He leaned in and cupped his mouth with his left hand as though he wanted to let me in on a secret.

'I tell you something. You know what Buddha teach? When self advance', his hands now tapping his heart and then extending towards me, 'ten thousand thing retreat' he said, performing a gesture with his hands that was supposed to mimic an explosion of some sort. He continued, 'When self retreat', his hands now circling back to his heart space, seemingly collecting all the air on their way, 'ten thousand things advance'. No gesture. Just a head shake. For the first time since I laid eyes on him, his smile disappeared. He almost looked scared at the thought of what he had just said…and then he broke out in laughter.

I did not quite get his message, to be honest, but it stuck with me, so I went to Google it back home. 'Buddhism, 10,000 things' is what I typed into the search engine. Turns out that the actual Buddhist teaching goes like this: 'The self advances and confirms the ten thousand things is called delusion. That the ten thousand things advance and confirm the self is called enlightenment'[vii]. Still quite a lot to unpack here! I am no Buddhist teacher – hard to believe, I know – so I can only pass on the knowledge I acquired through our good old friend the internet. Apparently, what the teaching means to express is that when we assume to know and master the world, that is, the ten thousand things around us, we are delusional. But when we understand that in the face of ten thousand things, that is, the world around us, we are actually incredibly insignificant, we can view every experience as a teachable moment. This Buddhist teaching urges us to go from believing we are the expert or the master to being humble enough to understand we are actually always a student and a beginner.

So what does cultivating this 10,000-things-mindset have to do with the monk's radiating joy and child-like ease? Like I said, I am not qualified to pass on Buddhist teachings, but what I take from this mindset for myself is that when we step out of knowing-mode into learning-mode, we are able to surrender to things being the way they are. We don't assume we can force a new reality on something we experience, and we view experiences, especially emotional ones, as more neutral, less significant, as something we can approach with more ease. I have tried to cultivate this mindset and actively check myself to apply it in my day-to-day experiences. I can only recommend you try it, too.

It works wonders for equipping yourself to handle discomfort. It allows you to be more relaxed about negative external shocks. With the ease that comes from surrendering to what is in front of you or coming up inside of you as a reaction to these external experiences, tell your mind, 'I can handle this'. Don't tell it 'Everything will be ok', expecting your external circumstances to change your inner reality. Say, 'I can handle this' and take responsibility. Because I have come to know my self inside out, I am at ease with my inner reality, and I am thus able to respond to my environment and take responsibility for bettering my state of mind. I am response-able. It takes a while to really cultivate this mindset and establish a firm and reliable practice of it. If I could recommend one thing to do, one strategy to get there, I would tell you to humble yourself! Actively. Every day. Be grateful. Be thankful for the gift of your body, your brain, your heart. Be thankful for what your body does for you every day and nourish it accordingly – with food, with books, with exercise, with anything that replenishes your energy.

If you are gifted with extraordinary stamina and can easily perform at high levels in athletics, celebrate that. If you have a photographic memory, cherish that. If you have a body that is healthy and equipped to bear children, be grateful for that. I know it sounds so cheesy and esoteric, but honestly, be grateful and humble. Become aware of the wonders a healthy and functional body holds and the millions and billions of things that had to go right in our formation for us to turn out with all the functions and abilities we have. Let's just try and cultivate an awareness for the preciousness of life (yeah, cheese-balling again, I know). To make it less cheese-ball and more hard facts, let's take a look at some numbers: There is an estimated 295 exabytes of data floating around the world. That equals 29,500,000,000,000,000,000,000 pieces of information! That's all the grains of sand on Earth multiplied by 315. And although that's pretty much humungous, it is still less than one per cent of the information that is stored in our DNA. Things as we know them have been around for some 14 billion years, and we had nothing to do with that. It's really healing to understand that not everything is about us. If you can't buy a plane ticket to the Amazon, do the next best thing and watch a jungle documentary on Netflix. Just marvel at it. Try to lean away from the noise for a moment and just be with your self, appreciating…

***

A few months back, I was dating a guy who asked me a lot of philosophical questions, like what are you most thankful for in your life thus far? Or what would you change about the way your parents raised you? If I were your closest friend, what would be the one thing you'd like to know about me? He also asked me 'What makes you someone I should date? What is the one special thing about you that should make me be with you?' He did not ask me this because he wanted me to sell myself to him or for me to convince him of my worth; he just wanted to know what my perspective on my own uniqueness was. I told him that I don't feel like it's my place to define or judge that because I believe it is not at my discretion to determine what qualities someone should value in me. He didn't let me off the hook quite that easily though and insisted I at least hint at an answer to the question.

Now that we're just between us, I can speak freely. The answer I would have given him would be a summary of all my beliefs I wrote about in this chapter, concluding with how all of it feeds my approach to relationships: from the knowledge and broader perspective we gain about our self through introspection and self-examination emerges modesty and the acknowledgement of our own limitedness and imperfection. This modesty and acknowledgement of our limitedness plants a self-critical corrective in us that helps us recognise the prejudices we have about others, preparing us to question the absolute rightness (and righteousness) of our assumptions about the people around us. It is precisely this conscious recognition and consideration that feeds my approach to relationships: I have the utmost respect for the person I am with because I believe everyone does the best with what they've got, and I want to cherish their right to being their own person, living life the way they deem best. As we talked about in the beginning of this chapter, we want to avoid searching for our own identity and source of self-worth in our partners. Of course, the same goes the other way around; their identity shouldn't be defined by us. I want to share a beautiful poem that puts this into the best words I have yet come to read:

> *You were born together, and together you shall be forevermore.*
>
> *You shall be together when the white wings of death scatter your days.*
>
> *Ay, you shall be together even in the silent memory of God.*
>
> *But let there be spaces in your togetherness,*
>
> *And let the winds of the heavens dance between you.*
>
> *Love one another, but make not a bond of love:*
>
> *Let it rather be a moving sea between the shores of your souls.*
>
> *Fill each other's cup, but drink not from one cup.*

Give one another of your bread, but eat not from the same loaf.

Sing and dance together and be joyous, but let each one of your be alone.

Even as the strings of the lute are alone though they quiver with the same music.

Give your hearts, but not into each other's keeping.

For only the hand of Life can contain your hearts.

And stand together yet not too near together:

For the pillars of the temple stand apart,

And the oak tree and the cypress grow not in each other's shadow.

Kahlil Gibran, On Marriage

This mutual freedom and respect described so poetically by Gibran (and less poetically by me throughout this chapter) is essential for relationships – romantic and platonic alike. Unerring respect for one another, holding each other in high esteem and trusting that both of you are doing the best with what you've got. When two individuals share a life together, different values and perspectives are bound to become an issue of contention. When things get rough, really consider who your partner is at their core. Ask yourself, at whom or what their actions are really directed at. Contextualise their behaviour. What are their past experiences that may influence the way they act now? What are their needs that they're trying to fulfil? Just try to understand them and give room for questioning your assumptions about them.

Close to the end of my last relationship, I started to suffer from my boyfriend's behaviour. It felt confusing that even though I was unsatisfied, I did not want to leave him. I was not blinded by love or scared of being alone. Rather, I was reflecting on my feelings, and I created room for understanding that just because I had problems with some things that happened between us, it didn't mean my problem was with who he was as a person. Despite everything I suffered from, I could not imagine leaving him because he was exactly the person he needed to be. He was not supposed to be a certain person for me. He was supposed to be for himself. Issues arose out of how he translated his intentions into actions. At the time, those actions didn't work so well for me. I saw his efforts to be better, and I saw that he suffered more from himself than I ever would. In other words, I saw his intentions, I saw who he was, and I loved who he was. All of it. That made it worthwhile for me to stick around and stay with him while he worked on making the necessary changes to his behaviour.

I understood that his behaviours stemmed from his inability to follow his intuition, which made him feel lost and unable to trust himself, along with the fact that he tended to overthink, the fact that he was still scared to trust me with everything one hundred percent, and many other things he was dealing with and healing from. I see the management of these struggles and developing ways to deal with them better as part of a relationship – a journey together. I think it's part of the way we get to know each other. If you want to really stay with someone for the long run, plenty of rough phases will come up. I don't think the way to go would be to take a break every single time things get tough or to retreat to being by ourselves and dealing alone with the issues that affect both us and our partners. As a couple, you just try to ride the waves together. Sometimes, they last hours, sometimes days, sometimes weeks, sometimes maybe even months or years. But the point is that they pass, and in the end, what counts is that you're doing all this with the person you want to be with.

Even during the times of struggle in our relationship, I saw my partner's efforts. We had straining issues, and I needed those to be solved for me to continue to be happy in the relationship. I want to make clear that I didn't need my partner to change; I needed his behaviours towards me to change. I challenged him to outgrow himself in certain areas of his life so that we could stay together. (He did the same for me, by the way.) He really tried to make things work, never once let me doubt that he loved me, but in the end, it came down to the fact that he had a long path of personal development to go before he'd reach a place of personal fulfilment from where our relationship could be sustained. I think he wasn't ready for the process of growth and transformation that 'we' needed; he had to tend to growing and transforming himself as an individual first, so eventually, things ended between us.

What I'm trying to say is that we *should* challenge each other to grow, and we absolutely *have to* state when we need change to happen because we are suffering. But we can't have expectations about the speed of change or the way our partners go about their transformation. We have to give each other the room to grow, and that means not putting restraints in terms of requirements and expectations on each other, forcing our partners to morph into something we want them to be instead of something they choose to be. It takes endurance and commitment and dedication and hard work. But I want to urge every-one to never give up in the face of the first little obstacle. Not even in the face of big obstacles whose roots may run deep into the personality of either you or your partner. Give each other time to build something for yourself in the partnership. Go back to the beginning of this chapter and remind yourself of what we talked about: we have to make choices about what is fair to ask of our partner and what is our own job to provide for ourselves. Both require investments, and we have to empower ourselves to make conscious decisions about the areas in which we invest in our partners and in what areas we should invest in ourselves and our personal networks. Whatever it is that we ask of our partners, whatever it is that we yearn for, it needs to be cultivated. And continuously so. Neither fulfilment nor bliss nor love are constant states of enthusiasm. They arise from ac-tions and behaviours that need to be fed with a permanent sense of resilience and a continuous pattern of devotion.

Without the bedrock of such earnest and unerring respect, no relationship will stand a chance. I guess that's the answer to the question of why I think someone should date me. I won't ever try to change my partner or take away their room to grow. That's what I want to pass on here: Simply abide by your part-ner's difference, remind yourself that you love this person with good reason, respect each other and believe in each other's good intentions. Don't ever be the reason for your partner to settle for less than they want to be simply because who they are doesn't fit with your idea of who they should be for you. Be your partner's inner peace for the decisions they make, be part of their drive, part of their confidence, part of their trust in themselves. Trust that you're not going to lose the 'us' over becoming two individual 'I's.

If you see them make an effort and doing their best with what they've got, it shows they're dedicated and that they want to work on building something together. I believe that the least we can do for our partner, then, is to show patience, appreciation and the same dedication they demonstrate for us. You don't want to give your partner the feeling that there is no winning with you. That'd be the beginning of the end, and it'd be our fault, not our partner's and what we perceive as the shortcomings in them. So – let's not ask from our partners to add something to our life that is in fact essential for *us to provide to ourselves*. Let's not ask our partner to take on a role that we defined for them. Let's not ask our partner to provide us with something we need, something our happiness or joy depends on. Let's ask of them to accompany us in our development, ask of them to be our inner peace, our safe haven, ask of them to set our head straight because after all they're the ones who know us best. Let them be the frame to our life, but not the content. The frame that makes our metaphorical artwork a unified whole, providing structure and protection for something that still stands and matters on its own.

This brings us to chapter two: to give. Enjoy the ride!

The Battle of Giving or
Staying Independent

If we manage to become our most resourceful selves and grow, becoming able to provide essential resources to ourselves rather than asking others to provide them for us, we also enable ourselves to give from a place of abundance. Our resources to give to others will be self-replenishing and sustainable. In many ways, I believe the key to being a good partner and building long-lasting relationships is exactly here: asking for nothing (because you provide for yourself) and being able and willing to give everything (because you are resourceful). Now, bear with me here for a second. I'm not talking about the kind of stuff we see all over the movies and that we read about in romance novels. I'm not talking about sacrifice. Giving someone everything is very different from giving everything up for someone.

Romantic sacrifice is somewhat idealised in our culture. The movies teach us that love comes with extra burdens, extra worries, extra responsibilities and extra sacrifices. Those are the metrics for what a 'successful relationship' is. The more you have to endure to get love, the more special and worth-it that love is. That's pretty screwed up. It's screwed up to be taught that we have to forego parts of ourselves to secure our relationships and to not lose our partners. So the kind of giving I'm talking about is not the kind where you do it out of obligation and self-sacrifice, but the kind where you do it out of respect and love. Pure and loyal and noncontingent, not expecting anything in return.

Giving is not about you. Don't see a relationship as an investment and expect an ROI (return on investment). In business, the concept of ROI is used to determine whether an investment is worthwhile or not. If the return is expected to be high, then the investment is justified. If the return is expected to be negative, you might want to reconsider before investing. In relationships, we invest anything from time to energy to money to our personal development, and we expect the ROI to be love, admiration, care, security and so on. We're somehow taught that the person we love deserves to be given our all. We're supposed to invest everything we have into our relationships to get the most precious reward of all: love. In my experience, there is usually a fundamental difference between giving someone *all that you have* and giving them *what they need*. And it is this distinction that makes all the difference between sustaining and destroying our relationships with what we give[viii]. We might give our partner all of our free time because we think that's what they deserve and want, hence what they need. What they really need, however, may in fact be alone time to free up the emotional resources they can provide to our relationship. Maybe we sacrifice our career to enable our partner to pursue their goals because we think what they need is for us to provide them with the optimal, barrier-free conditions to advance professionally. Maybe, however, what they really need to feel successful is overcoming the very barriers we're trying to break down for them and still managing to sustain our relationship at the same time.

Giving our partners all we have easily leads to us expecting that they demonstrate gratitude for our sacrifices, that they love us more, treat us better, cherish the relationship more and never leave us because, obviously, they can't answer to our huge investment and sacrifice by dumping our sorry asses. These expectations create imbalance and frustration. What usually happens is that either the partner on the receiving end will eventually feel bored and suffocated, or the partner on the giving end will eventually realise that all their giving remains unreciprocated and then feel like a fool. What was the intention behind all this sacrifice again? Oh, right, it was securing the base of our relationship and not losing our partner. Seems like that didn't work out so well...

With our way of life nowadays, it has become increasingly difficult to choose in what or whom we invest in the first place. We can meet millions of people at the click of a button or, rather, the swipe of a screen. With the number of choices available to us, it has become increasingly difficult to commit or – god forbid – to settle. What if someone better is still out there? What if I meet someone tomorrow who is even better looking, makes even more money, drives an even faster car or loves me even better? Being exposed to so much choice, so many possibilities makes us doubtful. So as rational decision makers, it would only make sense for us to delay making choices to further assess the possible alternative outcomes, right? We're faster to think that we might have made the wrong choices, so more and more often, we avoid making choices altogether.

Committing to one person becomes less and less attractive. We can find our partners anywhere in the world now, and we're scared to settle for someone who is not an appropriate equivalent or counter-value for what we embody. As societies, we have become utter capitalists of human interaction, living in a time of notorious dissatisfaction. Many parts of our economic and social systems rely on the fact that we create an ever-growing demand for everything that we produce. Growth depends on demand never being saturated. Generally, I welcome the creative destruction and constant development that is at the heart of this system. However, in relationships, it is toxic. When there is genuine love and affection, the basic sustenance of our relationships should not feel laborious or be viewed as something we approach with the mindset of a stockbroker.

Many of us are eager to give, but we don't always do so with kindness and graciousness. Expectations and later resentment for unfulfilled expectations can cause huge relationship problems. As I emphasised in the previous chapter, I believe that unerring respect for one another, holding each other in high esteem and trusting that both of you are doing the best with what you've got is essential for relationships. From this respect comes everything else – trust, patience, perseverance, leaving each other room to grow, as well as the noncontingent and loyal giving out of love and respect.

Without that bedrock of respect underneath us, we will doubt each other's intentions. We will judge each other's choices and encroach on each other's independence. We will feel the need to hide things from one another for fear of criticism. And this is when the cracks in the edifice begin to appear.

Of course, relying on a bedrock of respect means *showing* respect, but that is too superficial. Just showing respect isn't enough. You have to *feel* it deep within you. Maybe you deeply and genuinely respect your partner for their work ethic and patience. Maybe you respect them for their creativity, their intelligence and their core values. Maybe this leads to you always wanting to hear what they have to say – even if you don't agree with them – because you respect their opinion. Hopefully, you want to enable them to have some free time within your insanely busy lives because you respect how they choose to spend their time and who they spend it with. This is the kind of respect I'm talking about. The kind of respect which means that we can mutually feel safe sharing our deepest, most intimate selves with one another. That's the kind of giving and receiving we want to be cultivating.

***

To have such deep, genuine, unerring respect for someone can only stem from having the same kind of respect for our self. In the previous chapter, we talked a lot about becoming our most resourceful selves, being truly in touch with ourselves and thus being able to take responsibility for our inner realities. With developing that mental culture comes the struggle of continuously calibrating and figuring out what we are supposed to take responsibility for and what is out of our hands or what is other people's responsibility. Lord, grant me the serenity to accept the things I cannot change, the courage to change the things I can and the wisdom to know the difference, right?

I've not always been very successful at navigating among what I need to do, what I don't need to do and what I can't do. I tended to not have the wisdom to know the difference between the things I was responsible for and the things that were other people's responsibility. Especially when it came to handling conflict; I always felt responsible for approaching the situation with understanding and reflection, trying to identify and correct the wrongdoings on my part that lead to those conflicts.

Back in high school, there was some kind of campaign the student council ran every year for Valentine's Day. Sometimes, you could anonymously send roses to people you liked, or you could buy them chocolates or something cutsie like that. One year, we could write little notes to people, and someone dressed up as cupid would deliver them on Valentine's Day. That year, I was 14 or 15, I received a card from a girl in my class. She sent cards to all her friends with short greetings and cute messages. I wasn't part of her circle of friends, so I was really surprised to receive a card from her. The card said something along the lines of:

I hope you'll become more confident to be who you are. When problems arise, you always seek the fault in yourself and try to take responsibility for someone else's shitty behaviour. You should stop doing that. But you know what...it's also a quality that too few people have. It makes you more human than any of us.

I'm struggling with 'trying to stop doing that', that is, not taking responsibility for someone else's shitty behaviour, even today. But I assume that distinguishing between what we are and aren't responsible for is one of the greatest enigmas of human existence. As the course of our lives change and our biographies take shape, we have to continuously reassess where our responsibilities lie. This can be a challenging and unpleasant process, if we do it earnestly and conscientiously. We have to cultivate the capacity and willingness to continuously self-examine and introspect. A huge amount of experience and basically a lifetime of maturation are necessary for us to gain the ability to see the world and our place in it realistically – and from there on realistically assess our responsibilities[ix]. Life becomes a constant negotiation with the self.

Psychologists have long dealt with these brain-racking questions. A lot of research has been done on the sense of responsibility that we develop in the early stages of our life and how this sense changes with time and experience. Children, for example, will almost always take responsibility for certain deprivations that they experience and do not yet understand. Children who are not loved by their parents, for example, will probably assume they are unlovable rather than understanding that it is actually their parents who are deficient in their capacity to love. It is difficult for children to blame their parents because they are a child's point of reference for correct behaviour. Wrongdoing on the parents' part is not yet part of children's reality, and their only frame of reference for right and wrong behaviour is set by the feedback they get from their parents.

When I was about nine years old, my parents divorced. I think it's pretty common for the children of divorcees to feel at least partly responsible for their parents splitting up or for causing turmoil in the family. That was not so much the case for me. I didn't feel responsible for my parents' divorce, but I had other responsibility issues concerning my relationship with my father. We never had a very close relationship; I don't remember him being around much. He had always been a smoker, and because my mum didn't want him to smoke in the house, my father put up an armchair in the garage and made it his area of retreat. He'd come home from work, we'd all have dinner together, and then, he'd disappear into the garage and spend the entire evening there. Five days a week. I remember that on the weekends, he'd sometimes sleep until eleven a.m., sometimes even two p.m., which for me was a sign of total laziness, neglect and disinterest in his family life.

I was not very upset when our parents told us they were going to divorce. I was lacking the intellectual capacity to understand fully what them getting a divorce meant. I could not yet fathom the idea that being a family didn't mean we all have to live together. But on a purely emotional level, I was not upset that my father was leaving us. I was always embarrassed by him when we were in public together (though at age nine, I didn't understand what it was about him that made him different from the 'regular' dads). I didn't feel very comfortable being around him when he *was* there. So in short, I didn't mind him leaving. And I felt guilty about that.

For the first years after the divorce, my sisters and I spent our school breaks with our father. Whether we wanted to or not, our mum made us go. He moved back to Germany after the divorce, while we were still living in London, so we flew over there two to three times a year. He had a small apartment in a rundown neighbourhood of Berlin. I didn't feel comfortable going there, and I always wondered why he didn't think about the fact that his children would come to visit when he chose the apartment. The inside of the apartment was cleanish but messy. Some laundry was always piling up in the bathroom, and a few dishes remained unwashed in the kitchen; it smelled of cold cigarette smoke (because with my mum gone, he could smoke inside – although he didn't do so when we were around), and the furniture that came with the apartment was ugly and didn't fit together. It just wasn't a very homey place, which was of course worsened by the fact that I didn't feel comfortable being around my father and that my mum was far away.

Being the oldest of three, I felt responsible for my younger sisters having a clean apartment where dishes weren't piling up and where everything was clean. Technically, that should have been our father's responsibility, him being the adult, the parent and all. But I was very much incapable of leaving this responsibility to him and thought I needed to take care of things being done the right way, like they were at home with our mum. My sisters didn't complain about how our father's place looked. They didn't ask for me to do something about what I perceived as a mess. They didn't feel uncomfortable. But I couldn't stand the thought of my sisters living like this – even though cleaning and tidying up my father's apartment was not my responsibility at all. I did what I recall to be a deep cleaning (remember, I was like ten years old) of the bathroom, and every morning and evening I'd wash up and clean the kitchen.

One morning, I piled all the dishes up in the kitchen sink and left them there to soak. In the meantime, I went to get dressed or something like that; in any case I left the dishes unattended. My father must have needed to use the sink in the bathroom, but one of my sisters was occupying it at the time, so he went to the kitchen to use the sink there. I heard the dishes rattle first and then him angrily calling me to the kitchen. He was mad at me for blocking the sink and asked how I could do something that stupid. I didn't even have a chance to reply. He just dismissed me with the words, 'No wonder I can never love you. You do things exactly like your mother'.

So that was that.

I struggled for many, many years with the idea that I was unlovable to my father. Instead of considering it his incapability of loving me, his child, I accepted the responsibility for having to become more lovable in his eyes. So I tried over and over again to build and improve our relationship (after all, I saw he was well capable of being a loving dad to my sisters, so I had to assume that it was about me personally). Disappointment after disappointment, my mum had to put my broken heart back together as she wondered more and more why I still kept up my hopes for a good father–daughter relationship, even though I had come to know very well over the years that my father was never going to change in his behaviour towards me. In her eyes, my feeling hurt, angry, enraged, betrayed, abandoned, rejected and so on did not make sense. I was not supposed to feel this way, apparently. Not anymore. Not after I should have learned that there is a reality to be dealt with that included me not having a relationship with my father. What resulted from this was that I took on all the responsibility for our relationship not working. However, I also took on all the responsibility for feeling the way I felt, considering myself too weak to move on from the disappointments and the pain, not tough enough to accept that I just wouldn't be loved by my father.

In the end, that latter responsibility was what pulled me out of my misery. My mum's reaction towards my struggle may not have been the most sensitive one, but it surely made me reflect on my place and my responsibility in the conflict with my father. It still took me years to understand that it was up to him to assume and stay in his role as the parent and that it was his responsibility to be a father before it was my responsibility to be a daughter. But I learned it eventually. I started being more and more assertive towards him. I started telling him that I felt uncomfortable around him and that I didn't want to visit him anymore. I started to tell him when I didn't want him around for certain events, like birthdays or meeting my first boyfriend. Even though my mother made clear to me that it was time for me to get over all the disappointments already, she also didn't approve of me shutting him out. I see how you may get confused here; imagine how I felt as a kid getting such mixed messages. For years, the message I got from her was 'take responsibility for your wellbeing and stop accepting responsibility your father's deficiencies', and suddenly, that was wrong, too. I stuck with my decision though because I felt better this way. It also allowed me to communicate to my father what I thought had to be addressed between us because I wasn't afraid to break our relationship anymore. I started accepting that most of it was already broken, and if there was a chance for things to be fixed, it would have to be up to him to do so. I still held out hope for that to happen, though, for him to finally accept his responsibility. But at the very least, I let go of my responsibility for the whole conflict.

On my seventeenth birthday, I told him that I did not want him to come to our house for the celebration. He accepted that but asked me to at least have breakfast with him the next day. I didn't want to, but my mum made me go. We met in a café and sat outside on the patio. The atmosphere was tense and awkward. He asked me to lay everything on the table that had been bothering me throughout the years. He wanted me to explain to him 'why I hated him' and what he had done wrong to cause all my resentment towards him. The fact that he even framed his question that way and the fact that he claimed to have no idea what he could possibly have done wrong to deserve his daughter hating him already led to me wanting to get up and go home. But like I said, I held out hope that he'd finally accept his responsibility and turn over a new leaf, allowing us to start over. So I started explaining things. And he dismissed everything I told him as either my own misconceived exaggerations or my mother's lies. None of the things I talked about even remotely moved him to admit that he had done something wrong. He simply refused to take responsibility for anything. Even today, that is the reason I can't forgive him, accept him and move on. The conversation turned ugly; I started crying, and he started yelling, all while sitting on the patio of that café in the centre of Berlin. Eventually, he stood up and left. In the middle of the conversation, in the middle of me crying, he just stood up. And left. I called my mum in tears, telling her that he left me sitting in the café, and I had no money to pay for the spread he ordered. She came to pick me up, paid the bill and took me home…

My father considers this conversation 'our big talk that cleared everything up'. I still don't understand how two peoples' perceptions of the same situation can be so utterly different.

When I was eighteen and in college, I finally pulled the rip-cord after yet another huge disappointment and told him via email that I did not want to speak to him again until I got over the trauma and disappointment of the past ten years:

> *Hi.*
>
> *Please stop calling. There is a reason that I don't answer the phone when you call.*
>
> *I can't keep crying all day when your behaviours disappoint me and when I can't cope with the fact that our relationship is not the father-daughter-relationship it should be. I have to get over it now and that won't work as long as we continue to be in contact.*
>
> *It surprises me time and again that your behaviour still bothers me this much and has such huge effects on me, but it's just the way it is and it's breaking me apart, so I cannot be in contact with you anymore.*
>
> *I can well imagine that this makes you feel bad and you feel you're being treated unfairly, because I'm only*

speaking up now. It probably seems like my decision came out of nowhere, but I've thought about this for a long time and finally have to make this decision.

I do not want to talk about it anymore. We had enough talks and still nothing has changed.

As I said, I must get to a point where I do not mind what happens between us and in order to get there, I do not want to have any contact.

Do not think this is easy for me. I'm crying again, but I think it's better this way.

You see how even after everything that happened, I still felt guilty for not wanting to talk to him. I still felt responsible for his emotions, the way I made him feel by making this decision for myself.

Generally, responsibility appears to be closely connected to guilt[x]. The feeling of guilt usually kicks in when we feel as though we transgressed against some sort of value system. These values are not always well defined or obvious, but they are either what we have defined as our personal moral standard or can also be some form of social command that may not be explicitly established anywhere but that most people seem to follow pretty closely. We'll talk more about values later on in the book. For now, we need the concept of values to understand that guilt and responsibility are confused when we question whether our behaviour towards others was in fact justified by our value system or whether we should be responsible for other people's emotional responses to our behaviour.

As such, guilt is a self-critical emotion and implies a negative moral self-evaluation. So from a great deal of introspection and reflection, which we discussed and encouraged in chapter one, stems modesty and the acknowledgement of our own limitedness on the one hand, but also a tendency for our self-critical corrective behaviour that questions our decisions and actions a little too harshly on the other hand. In accepting responsibility for our inner reality and cultivating response-ability, we also accept responsibility or the power to transgress our norms and, thus, our potential to harm others, thwart others' goals and so forth. We are adamant in accepting responsibility to handle this power with care. So by feeling guilty, we're fast to perceive the emotional response other people have towards our actions as the effect of our (willingly) misused power in being harmful and violating the standards of our moral self. The result is that we look to ourselves first to identify fault or blame in a conflict – just like my classmate pointed out to me in her

Valentine's Day card – so we might place responsibility where it doesn't belong: in our own hands.

Guilt implies viewing ourselves as responsible for the fault and thus is likely to motivate self-punitive or reparative behaviours. This means that guilt motivates us to accept responsibility for fixing a situation or making sure we will never do such a terrible thing again. It triggers perspective-taking and empathetic concern, perhaps to an extent that results in a certain degree of self-destruction. By considering others' needs and concerns and seeing the consequences of our actions through their eyes (all good qualities that I encourage you to cultivate!), we may compensate for the other person's limitedness to adequately deal with a situation. In addition, we may lose faith in our own value system and the idea that our behaviours may have in fact been an adequate reaction to someone else's wrongdoings.

In the previous chapter, I noted that it is essential for relationships to be built on unerring respect for one another, holding each other in high esteem and trusting that both of you are doing the best with what you've got. I wrote that in times of conflict, we should consider who the other person is at their core to contextualise their behaviour. I still stand by all of this. I just want to raise awareness to the fact that we have to do so within reason. It's good to factor the other person's background and feelings into our choices that concern them. But after all the contextualising and rationalising may come a time when we have to admit that some things are just plain shitty. And it's not our responsibility to fix this. Looking back at the examples I gave from my own life, it was neither my responsibility to fix my father's shitty behaviour, nor was it my responsibility to compensate for any of my ex-boyfriend's behaviour. I do, however, consider it my responsibility to find a way to deal with their behaviours and not ask of them to change so that I can feel better. But it's not my responsibility to hang in there forever and adjust to their behaviours, which is harmful to me, just to not hurt *their* feelings. To put it frankly, don't blame a clown for behaving like a clown, but do ask yourself why you're still going to the circus. But on a serious note - It's not our responsibility to save someone from bad feelings that their own behaviour caused.

In fact, not only is it not our responsibility, it's also simply not possible. We can't give others salvation. The key to someone's 'salvation' is their own mental growth. As friends, lovers, partners, parents or children, we cannot compensate for the work others have to put in for their own happiness and satisfaction. We can and have to take responsibility for *our* role in a relationship, but not for the role of the other person involved. Even our greatest efforts to nurture someone's mental growth is doomed to fail if they don't take their part of the responsibility for it. This may sound harsh at first, but what I learned – the hard way – is that attempting to love, nurture and enrich someone who is incapable of benefitting from your efforts is a waste of your time and energy. Genuine love and care is precious, and those who are capable of accepting and reciprocating it know that they have to take responsibility for appreciating and returning other people's giving. And accepting this is a huge condition for building the unerring respect for yourself that we have talked about.

In this way, when we commit to someone, we can commit our actions and good intentions to them. But we cannot commit our thoughts, feelings and perceptions to the other. Hell, we can't even commit to ourselves to always be in control of our thoughts, feelings and perceptions, so how could we possibly feel responsible for committing our thoughts and feelings to other people? This all-consuming giving that is commonly associated with committing to someone is not love. It's parasitism[xi]. Of course, people are afraid to commit to or settle with someone if they assume this means giving up all their ability to choose and all their freedom. Committing to someone is being perfectly capable of living without them but *choosing* not to do so anyway. As such, love and relationships in general are not only pure and loyal giving, but they are also judicious and thoughtful withholding. Decidedly and responsibly calibrating where to draw boundaries and preventing each other from fully immersing into one another is needed because such immersion seeks to receive rather than to give (remember our discussion of expectations and ROI in the beginning of this chapter). Seeking only to receive and expecting an ROI from our investments into our relationships nourishes infantilism rather than growth. It works to trap and constrict rather than to liberate. Ultimately, it destroys rather than building people and relationships.

To be capable of that – genuine love, pure and loyal giving without expecting anything in return and balancing it all out with thoughtful withholding - requires us to cultivate our own mental and emotional abundance, which is the self-replenishing resource we can give to others. This requires discipline. It requires introspection. It requires experience and maturation and a mindset of reflection and learning. To be able to feel the unerring respect for others that is at the basis of all this non-contingent and loyal giving we must first cultivate the same kind of deep, genuine, unerring respect for our self. To be able to choose when to withhold our resources from our partners, we have to understand that our great power to harm people and transgress moral red lines doesn't come with the responsibility to save everyone from hardship. Rather, our responsibility to reflect on ourselves, to respect ourselves and others deeply, to contextualise and to critically question our behaviours and as-sumptions comes with the power to make good decisions and give our self and others what they need.

The Battle of Taking or Connecting to Our Values

In the previous chapter, we talked about the difference between guilt and responsibility and how guilt usually stems from the perception of having violated our values. We also talked about the need to continuously recalibrate what we are and aren't responsible for. This chapter is dedicated to enabling ourselves to perform this task by connecting to our values.

It happens in a not-so-insignificant number of instances that I cannot wrap my mind around peoples' actions and reactions. Sometimes, when they're faced with challenges, the way people deal with these challenges seems to get them into more trouble rather than out of it. Or maybe not more trouble, but a different kind of trouble that often amounts to life-changing shit and catapults them into an abyss that they didn't need to fall into. At least that's what it seems like from my uninformed, outside perspective. Anyway, none of the people I see acting in incomprehensible ways are stupid. They're all bright and intelligent. But I wonder how they sometimes manage to manoeuvre themselves from screwed-up situations into absolutely dismal situations. I wonder what the rules are that govern each of these people's behaviour. It doesn't seem rational for them to have made some of the choices they have made. I guess we all know that humans act predictably irrational, but to this extent? There must be something underneath the rational thinking part of people. Something invisible that we may or may not be aware of that has an important impact on our behaviour and state of mind.

There is. People don't act logically: they act psychologically. I don't want to get too deep into the neuroscientific or psychological research focusing on identifying the emotional patterns underlying our day-to-day actions. However, I do believe it is incredibly important to find a way to make these invisible rules visible and to become conscious of them. The first step is becoming aware of the impact our invisible rules have on our mind. It's important to be radically true to yourself here. It may be hard, but if you have gotten through chapter one ok and grasped the notion of the shadow-self as well as the importance of accepting our entire wholeness – the good and the bad – then I have faith we'll get through this part as well.

Research reveals that there are six basic human needs[xii]. First, there is certainty or comfort. It describes our need to be in control of what happens to us and to have a reasonable amount of predictability of what's next. Of course, certainty is the antidote for risk, so the importance we give to our need for certainty will determine how we make choices about our jobs, finances, vacation plans and so forth.

Second, there is uncertainty or variety. Wait, we have two basic needs that are each other's exact opposite? Yup. That's the lovely human brain for you. Basically, as humans, while craving predictability, we also have a need for challenge, for thrill, for something to continuously train us to flex our muscle of dealing with the unforeseen.

Then, there is significance. We have a need for a sense of importance, of feeling needed or wanted. It may take forms of needing to feel special or have special meaning to someone or for something. It's a basic human need to feel *worthy*.

Fourth, there is the need for love and connection. To be loved by other human beings means that we get their approval and that we belong to something; this might be in the form of an intimate connection. However, you can also create the feeling of belonging or connection through, say, prayer or yoga or connecting to nature. This is another instance where one of our basic needs is in paradox to another, by the way: our need for significance contradicts our need for love and connection. If we pay too much attention to our individual significance, it may come at the cost of experiencing deep connections with fellow humans and experiencing pure love.

Fifth, humans have a basic need for growth. Some scholars refer to this as 'a need of the spirit'. The need for growth describes humans' craving to constantly improve themselves, to advance from their emotional, spiritual or intellectual status quo to new heights and new achievements. This probably has evolutionary reasons: if we don't grow, we stop adapting to the challenges of our environment. We stagnate and eventually die.

Sixth and last, there is the need for contribution, the need to give beyond ourselves, to care for, serve and protect others. Meaning in life doesn't come from what you're getting: it comes from what you're giving. I'm sure this is a trick of evolution, too. Maybe we keep our species alive, keep humanity alive, through the basic human need for a certain degree of altruism.

Each of these six needs will have a different priority for each of us. Some may value certainty over variety, significance over connection, contribution over certainty and so forth. Personally, I give a way below-average priority to my need for certainty and a little below-average priority to my need for variety.

To all other four needs, I give above average priority, especially to my need for significance. My most important driving force is growth, closely followed by significance and contribution, as well as love and connection. Deciphering your basic 'need code' gives you important insights into what your powers are and what your kryptonite is likely to be.

If love and connection are a more dominant need for you, like they are for me, you're likely very passionate and committed to all your relationships, whether with your partner, your family or your friends. Most likely, sharing comes natural to you, and people can count on your kindness, support and generosity through the good times and the bad. You give freely, but you also share other people's joys and sufferings. It's probably easy for you to build trust, even with people you just met, and you likely crave a feeling of belonging to something – a team, a social group, any kind of social ties really or maybe something more abstract, such as causes. You don't hesitate to put energy into the growth of your relationships.

Hopefully, this knowledge adds some perspective to the things you've been reading about me so far. It explains a lot about why, even as a kid, I was obsessed with belonging to the popular people; I gave so much importance to belonging to their group. The fact that I was able to let go of the strife for being something my classmates portrayed as 'worthy' doesn't mean I changed my underlying basic need. I don't think I really have the power to do that; the wiring for this has been etched in my brain since the day I was born. But I shifted my priorities. I gave more importance to being connected to my self rather than to people who would only like me if I forewent who I was. I prioritised belonging to a cause over belonging to an artificial concept of self-worth that my classmates defined. I stepped out of the metaphorical race for popularity and validation, found my own lane and proceeded to win.

This also explains why I have a lot of stamina – or stubbornness – for making my relationships work, even though rationally speaking, the circumstances sometimes really aren't promising. Stemming from the high priority I give to my basic need for growth, my main driving force, I tend to view relationships as something I can always improve at. I suppose it's pretty weird to view relationships as something I strive to 'perform better at', but if I'm being honest, that's what I do. I strive to understand more about human emotion, about where it originates from, why people act like they do, how I can go from giving everything I have to giving someone exactly what they need, understanding how to maximise the extent to which I factor the individual in front of me into the relationship and, finally, how to create the optimal balance between the 'I's and the 'us'. Even though to a certain extent it's weird to view relationships as something I aim to grow and improve at, it's also the source of devotion and commitment.

As devoted and committed as I am to my relationships, my devotion to my own improvement resulting from the high priority I assign to my basic need for growth will always make connecting with others a bit less important to me than nourishing the relationship I have with myself. I actually never noticed this, but apparently, I have a sort of lone-warrior vibe in the eyes of some; even people who are very close to me see me this way. Once, over dinner, my sisters and I were joking around about which spirit animal to assign each of us. I was totally surprised when they both agreed on assigning me the peacock – because I fight for myself, as they said. I was somewhat offended by this notion, especially because it felt like they view me as someone who doesn't care about others on her way 'up'.

It took me some research and a follow-up conversation with my sisters about what they meant exactly by saying that I 'fight for myself', but I eventually came to terms with it. It was a really teachable moment for me about what could be my kryptonite based on my prioritised basic needs. I started understanding that I have to show people more clearly that I recognise the need for light-heartedness and laughter and that mastering the delicate balance between being very connected to myself and not seeming unapproachable to others because I am so connected to myself is something I have to shift my focus to. Shortly after I had this conversation with my sisters, a psychologist came to our workplace to assess all of us on how resilient we are to stress, how prone to burnout we are and so forth. Part of his report on my psychological state said the following:

> *You appear to me as a person who has a very good grip on how to handle most situations, because you are sustainably in touch with yourself and conscious of your abilities. As a result, you appear to be particularly confident and usually bold and straight forward. Presumably, this way you exude a high degree of natural authority and dominance, so that sometimes you seem almost untouchable to others. Being concerned about others' critical assessment of you is a largely foreign concept to you. On the whole, this makes you handle*

(difficult) situations with such confidence and compe-
tence that your behaviour can sometimes be interpreted
as arrogant. Overall, what others think about you will
be less of a concern to you as you are at ease and sat-
isfied with yourself as a person and aware of your
strengths. If you are confronted with clearly worded
criticism about yourself, you will usually be able to
handle it without compromising your self-esteem. How-
ever, the risk for people who have as high a level of
self-confidence as you have, is that criticism will hardly
get offered, as feedback-givers are often afraid of it.

So yeah, I need to work on things. But the psychologist's words would never have resonated with me to their full potential if my sisters hadn't been the ones to first offer me the very criticism and honest feedback I needed to hear.

If we try to decipher the basic needs of the people around us and how these needs create the invisible rules that govern their behaviour, we can find answers as to why they make their choices and how they may have ended up in more precarious situations than the ones they were trying to get out of. Why, for example, can someone sacrifice the world for another person, even when they have been put through hell by that person? It could be because they're driven the most by their need for contribution. Someone may assign an extremely high value to caring for others, giving beyond themselves, always being the bigger person and not putting themselves first; this person may find grounding and balance in being everyone's rock, an island of stability in the shitstorms life puts us through. Being a calming presence and showing indestructible resilience for their own stress and for other people's burdens may be their greatest power and – not to be neglected – the image of their persona, the image of whom they want to see themselves as and whom they want the world to see in them (remember chapter one). They might want people to see them as someone extremely loyal, someone everyone can count on at all times, and they might want people to know that they view their giving and caring as something utterly normal and self-evident. A person like this may feed their need for significance by being outstandingly thoughtful and unconditionally caring.

Now, let a strong need for contribution be complemented by a strong priority for the basic need for love and connection. Maybe someone in this case values love and connection so highly that they would forego other parts of themselves – other needs and values – to create connections and show unconditional love to others, so much so that they value showing unconditional love even to people who deeply hurt them instead of making sure they walk out of a troublesome situation unscathed. If they didn't show unconditional love, they may fear they are portraying an image of themselves they would despise to embody and something that would make all the values attached to their high-priority needs seem like a farce. A person with these need priorities would connect to people around them by being a source of unconditional love. This type of person is probably excellent at seeing the individual in any situation. Never judgemental, they contextualise behaviour. Ever the compassionate carer, they rationalise people's actions. They take on other peoples' burdens to help them free up the capacities to find calm and balance. Unfortunately, as for all of us, their incredibly resourceful powers are also their kryptonite and their almost martyrised self-sacrifice in the name of love and contribution can manoeuvre them into self-made catastrophes.

Take another example. Often, I wonder why people around me don't voice their needs and emotions or speak up for themselves, suppressing their feelings and finding ways to deal with hardship rather than nipping it in the bud. Someone may be driven by their need for significance; they may have a strong need for a sense of importance, feeling needed and – most of all – wanted. Maybe, they are very good at acquiring the skills and knowledge that make them superior in a certain discipline. They might have spent years being very successful at what they do and have never met anyone not hailing their talent, not appreciating their hustle. There may come a moment when not experiencing appreciation happens for the first time. Someone, then, may not see them for who they are, or believe to be. Instead of receiving praise, they may receive criticism. What kicks in first and defines the invisible rules for someone's behaviour in this situation is hurt pride. If others don't see that this person is special and valuable, not easy to be replaced, this person certainly won't go grovel at other peoples' feet to claim the praise and approval they think they deserve. After all, for years, everyone in their surroundings, be it friends, family or colleagues, may have seen in them the special, talented person they know they are. So why doesn't everyone?

Combine this with a high-priority need for growth, and this person is likely to feel stuck and unhappy because they're presented with an unjust blockade that they can't break down with their skills and knowledge, which of course they wouldn't be able to break down because this barrier is entirely made up of human emotion. What their need for growth instils in them is to begin to look at themselves first when presented with a problem so that they can identify where they went wrong, where they underperformed or what they should have done better. Where were they not smart enough? When did they fail at something? Seeing the setback as a challenge to be mastered, they'll try to retreat into their mind and figure out a smart way to deal with the situation at hand. During this phase, they may suffer and struggle, but they'd rather entirely remove themselves from a situation than show what they perceive as their own weakness to someone who fails at appreciating and celebrating their uniqueness.

***

With each of the six basic needs comes a plethora of values that are attached to or are derived from them. Not only do these values make up the invisible rules that govern our behaviour, but they are the fabric out of which we each weave together our emotional parachute or, in other terms, the cement we build our emotional homes from. We feel comfortable in our emotional homes, and we retreat there to deal with the challenges life presents us. Becoming aware of our psychological architecture is a tremendous help to better assess our reactions to certain confrontations and to consciously and conscientiously come up with strategies to tackle these challenges better. It's a way to outsmart our rather primitive rapid-response system.

There is a simple method, called the iceberg model, to make our invisible governing rules visible. I learned – and eventually taught – this technique during my time working for an HR strategy consultancy. The technique enables us to explore the needs and values underlying our decisions or behaviours in a relatively simple four-step process. Consider the following example: At the office, you witness a manager assigning a task to a team member. The team member crosses his arms in front of his chest and says, 'No, you have to assign this task to someone else'. What the manager sees is one of her team members refusing to do his work. He displays a behaviour that suggests he is rejecting something she asked of him. The manager wants the task to be done by this particular team member, so she has to convince the employee of doing what she asked. As a witness to this conversation, you assume that the manager will now invoke her authority over her underling and simply force him to do as she says. She has to address his insubordination and remind him who the boss is. Instead of doing what you saw coming, however, the manager pulls over a chair, sits down with her team member and starts asking him questions.

'What feelings or thought made you reject carrying out the task I gave you?' she asks.

Her team member replies, 'Well, I won't be able to bring the task to completion. I could only offer an imperfect solution, and I feel like you ask too much of me'.

'Ok', the manager replies, 'I get that. But why do you believe so steadfastly that I want a perfect solution?'.

Her team member is fast to respond: 'It's not that I believe you want a perfect solution, it's more that I believe I have to deliver excellence in my work. I don't feel satisfied presenting you with a subpar result. However, I can only deliver high-quality results if I have enough time, and what you asked me to do simply doesn't allow for that'.

The manager responds, 'That's understandable. But what do you fear might happen if you don't deliver excellence in your work? What do you have to lose if you present me with an 80% solution?'

Her team member stops to think about this for a minute and finally replies, 'Well, I just want you to appreciate my work, and for that, I need to be able to fulfil my own standard and appreciate my work myself'.

'Ah', says the manager, 'now we're getting somewhere. Let me assure you that what I want from you and what I would appreciate is a first-draft solution to the task I assigned you. Come back to me with a basic result that can serve as food for thought for the full solution later in the process. We'll have more time to deliver excellence, but now is about getting started'.

The same scenario could have, of course, played out differently. Maybe the conversation would have looked more like the following:

'What feelings or thoughts made you reject carrying out the task I gave you?' she asks.

Her team member replies, 'I have a tonne of stuff to do. I don't have an overview of all my to-dos anymore, and I feel really pressured now that you're increasing my workload even more'.

'Ok', the manager replies, 'I get that. But why is it so important to you to have an overview of all your to-dos? Surely, someone will remind you of an approaching deadline if you forgot about something'.

Her team member is fast to respond: 'I need to be in control of my time and resources. If I lose the overview over my to-dos, I lose control'.

The manager responds, 'That's understandable. But what do you fear might happen if you let go of some of your control and trust that your colleagues will remind you of your deadlines in case you're about to miss them?'

Her team member stops to think about this for a minute and finally replies, 'I simply feel insecure if I don't have complete control. I need an overview of my tasks and peace of mind that I have everything on my radar to feel secure'.

'Ah', says the manager, 'now we're getting somewhere. This task I assigned you is extremely important and needs to be prioritised over your other to-dos. Let's take a look at your to-do list and find tasks we can deprioritise. I'll extend your deadlines on those'.

In whichever way this scenario plays out, the important thing to note is that the manager realised that to get her task completed, what she has to address is not her team member's insubordination, but rather his underlying need that feeds his convictions and values, which led to him rejecting to carry out the task. We can transfer this method to any setting and apply it to ourselves to understand our reactions to certain challenges. This can be done in four steps:

1) What is the *behaviour* we display right now?
2) What *thoughts or feelings* made us behave like this?
3) What *values, convictions or beliefs* are at the source of these thoughts and feelings?
4) What are our *needs* that account for these convictions, values and beliefs to be of such importance to us?

I want to quickly remind you of something we talked about in chapter one: what will sustainably solve our problems is the kind of action that demands introspection and paying attention to our inner reality, a real exploration of the root of what makes us feel, think and ultimately act a certain way when faced with a challenge or problem. We have to develop a mechanism to find out what the right action will be to deal with the external reality, in order to tend to our internal reality. The iceberg model can be your number one tool to achieve exactly that. The four questions guide you through your different levels of thinking: from the event level to the pattern level to the structure level and, finally, the mental-model level.

Behaviours are displayed at the event level. This is the level at which we perceive and process our environment, for example, walking up to your team member one day and having them reject carrying out a task you assigned to them. Although the problem could be solved simply by readjusting something on the event level, that is, addressing your employee's insubordination, the iceberg model challenges us to not only address the symptom, but rather to cure the disease by digging deeper through our levels of thinking.

If we look just below the event level, we find patterns. Similar events may have occurred over time, and they may be rooted in similar origins. In our example, the manager can only function as a trigger for her employee to access his pattern level by asking specific questions. Truly accessing the pattern level and uncovering patterns is the team member's job. When applying the iceberg method to ourselves, we assume both roles: asking the questions and providing the answers.

Below the pattern level lays the structure level, where we find the causes behind our patterns. The values, convictions or beliefs that make up our psychological architecture are located here and are often the product of what we're taught by our parents or educational institutions, our (unconscious) habits or our past experiences. There may not always be an explanation for why we believe in certain things or adhere to certain values, but looking at the mental-model level can shed some light on how our structure level came to be.

Understanding our mental-model also allows us to evaluate whether our values actually help us or rather make us stuck (like we saw in the three stories at the beginning of this chapter). Reflecting on the hidden rules that govern your behaviour with the methods described in this chapter sheds light on the values we hold dear and the metrics we use to assess our progress towards living by them. Maybe, as in our first example dialogue between the manager and her employee, we value excellence and measure it by how much our work is appreciated. Or maybe, as in the second example dialogue, we value security and measure it by the amount of control we have over a given situation. But what if we're choosing bad metrics for ourselves? Maybe, a better metric for measuring excellence is how many times our bosses entrust us with important tasks? Perhaps security is better measured by how much we are respected by others and thus have room to make mistakes? Here, the important aspect about our behaviour is not so much what is objectively true to outside observers, but rather how we see a situation, how we measure it and how we value it.

Accessing our mental-model level is the holy grail of introspection. Uncovering our basic-need-priority list is the key to understanding our every move, thought and feeling. Deciphering this code and putting the levels together by observing and tracking our driving forces, value structures and thinking patterns allows us to forecast and fully understand our behaviour in certain reoccurring situations. It significantly increases our response-ability, thereby allowing us to take responsibility for our inner reality. We grow and become better able to find strategies to react to conflicts or problems, all without being kicked out of our emotional homes. We can cultivate a certain degree of mental immunity by using these methods to manage our emotional responses to our external realities.

Discovering your shadows, uncovering the hidden rules that govern your behaviour and accepting your entire self ultimately culminates in being able to grow and learn from what triggers us emotionally and how to respond to it. We can train our responses to these emotional triggers after we reflect on them, eventually coming to understand them. It is equally important to come to terms with having certain thoughts and feelings as it is to find strategies to deal with them. Under no circumstances will we succeed at accepting our thoughts and feelings by telling ourselves that we're *not allowed* to use certain metrics to measure our value adherence or that the certain values that we cherish are inadequate. What we should ask ourselves, however, is how much certain things matter. Does it matter how much money I make? Does it matter how well I'm liked? Does it matter that I'm right all the time? In the face of the very influence we're trying to have on our environment by living by our values and in the face of the mark we want to make – the legacy we want to leave behind – what are the things that really matter? How do we really connect to our values and what are the reasons for which we do what we do?

Connecting to our values, staying independent and growing to become our most resourceful selves enables us to see ourselves as something bigger than ourselves. We can choose the values that stretch beyond serving our self. We can choose the values that are more complex and challenging than the immediate control we seek to have over the chaotic world around us. We become humble, as we talked about several pages ago, and understand that everything is not about us. We can find calmness and composure in understanding that we don't matter that much in the grand scheme of things. But we can also accept that we are allowed to take when we can't provide something by ourselves for ourselves. We can accept that we are allowed to withhold our giving for our own good when necessary and that we can expect others to accept the responsibility they should take. We don't have to be martyrs of our own value system. Closeness and independence can exist together, and

both qualities determine the health and happiness of our relationships.

And this brings us to chapter four: to share.

The Battle of Sharing or
Cultivating Resilience to Challenges

I believe that we learn what it means to be human from sharing and exchanging with other humans. Without contact with other people, exchanging and sharing with them, we cannot fully be ourselves. A human becomes human through other humans. And as Renaissance philosopher Pico della Mirandola helped us understand, human beings are the only creatures that are able to take an active part in constructing themselves – and their self[xiii]. We're part of a complex complementarity, part of a network that amplifies who we are. Sharing amplifies us. Our successes, our failures, our suffering, our joy. This amplification, this constant personal transformation, comes from the continuous gaining of new perspectives on being alive, enhancing our personal strength through confrontation and adversity; exploring and acting on new possibilities that we encounter through the interactions with our surroundings; learning from our experiences; and improving our relationships and deepening our perceptions and knowledge. Being fulfilled in life depends on both being sufficiently strong in our ideals and values and being sufficiently permeable to question our own ideals, even being inspired or transformed by the people around us.

There are many psychological and sociological theories around that posit that opening up to and sharing with our fellow humans allows us to experience positive emotions of belonging, being cared for and being worthy[xiv]. As we broaden our self through sharing with others, we build new emotional and behavioural repertoires that allow us to expand and improve our personal resources. We broaden our worldviews and open ourselves up to new possibilities that enable us to respond to our environment in more constructive and positive ways. We can move away from responding to our environment with urges to attack or flee and instead grow towards responding with the urge to explore, to savour and to integrate. As such, positivity begets positivity. Positive experiences and emotions through sharing promote the discovery of novel and creative approaches and solutions to dealing with our environment. Sharing helps us develop new ideas, forge new and closer social ties and thus build and enrich our personal resources – be they physical, intellectual, social and psychological – by serving ourselves a helping from the 'extended mind'[xv] that is our social environment.

In other words, our identities form as a response to our environmental contingencies because we have to build aids for the orientation in and for constant evaluation of our environment. This becomes possible only under the condition that there exists a mechanism of control that can anticipate environmental contingencies and that can react to them. Over the years, you probably have come to realise that we cannot consciously control our environment all the time. Control, in this case, can only be understood in relation to our own identity and that of all other identities. The social contexts and ties we *consciously* find ourselves in (i.e., we are aware of them) are our observable point of reference for 'reality' and create our expectations about and thus our control mechanisms for our environment. As individuals, we are embedded in a myriad of more or less stable, lasting and intensive social connections. In each of these connections, we might take on a different role. When we refer to the social context of our family, we might have the role or identity of son, mother, daughter, brother, uncle or grandma. In the social context of our work environment, we may define our identity as boss, team leader, coworker or support staff. In a less-intensive, short-lived social context such as the supermarket, we may define our identity as a customer. Only by being conscious of our different roles and the fact that we switch between them do our identities actually develop. The possibility of finding ourselves in various social contexts, being paired with the awareness that it is possible to change between various contexts and our respective identities, creates the very environmental contingency that is essential to the formation of our identity[xvi].

Considering all of this, our 'control' places the idea of 'our identity' in a reality that we are required to deal with via constant re-evaluation and repositioning. There has to be a conscious cognitive effort that we make to be aware of our 'switching' between social contexts. Even though it sounds complicated, our existence in manifold social contexts allows us to simplify and constrain the arbitrariness of our environment. In order to attempt to gain control or circumstantially reinterpret our identity, we need to be able to predict – or at least anticipate – our environment's reaction to our behaviour. And this is what I mean by saying 'sharing amplifies us' and that 'we become human through other humans'. The resonance we receive from other people opens up a possibility space that can show us everything that others believe we could be. With that, the self is offered a space to grow into. We identify with the conscious knowledge we have about ourselves, and we can only know ourselves in so far as we are mirrored by our surroundings.

Other people who take the time to pay attention to us move something in us, bring something to the surface and help us experience new aspects of our self. We orient ourselves mainly by observing and exploring our environment – our external circumstances. Like I mentioned in previous chapters, I find it quite ironic that the only real access we have to our *inside* is through *external circumstances.* But the way to build more internal personal resources is through our external experiences. The way to broaden our repertoire of thoughts and actions is to expose ourselves to adversity and challenge and engage in *constructive self-disclosure.*

Note that self-disclosure is not the same thing as self-exposure. Self-exposure involves revealing our darkness, while self-disclosure means exploring why there may be a lack of light in the first place. If that does not make sense, I'll try to make it more concrete. Self-exposure means revealing dishonest motives, feelings or behaviours. Admitting guilt, in a way. For example, it could be the confession of disturbing thoughts, the expressing of supressed feelings of hatred or the revelation of sexual improprieties. If you search for 'sharing yourself' on Quora, you'll find lots of questions such as, 'Do I have to tell my boyfriend how many people I've slept with?', 'I have fantasies of being tied up. Should I tell my girlfriend or keep quiet about them?' or even 'I had casual sex once when I was in college. Now I am in a serious relationship. Should I tell him?' (Not much further down the list, you'll find 'How common is it that a husband wants to share his wife?', but that's a whole other conversation on the topic of sharing). These are great illustrations of self-exposure – and of what sharing *does not* mean. Sharing or self-disclosure is not so much about expressing suppressed feelings, but rather, it is about exploring the motives behind suppressing them in the first place. Instead of revealing our secrets, it's about exploring how we became so secretive to begin with.

A secret wish inherent in all of us is to escape the gravity of the interpersonal and elevate our self to the greater heights of a magnificence that is rooted in independence, maybe a certain deviance or 'otherness'. And this is only understandable. However great the positive effects of sharing our being and disclosing our self, sharing can be challenging, especially our emotions and deep inner thoughts. It lays bare our innermost parts and makes us vulnerable to being challenged in the way we view the world, vulnerable to being attacked or maybe even manipulated. To cultivate greater flexibility and resilience to adversity and to allow ourselves to function optimally and flourish, we have to overcome this fear of vulnerability. Constructive self-disclosure and sharing with other humans is key to growth and longevity; beauty and goodness; robustness and resilience; and generativity and complexity.

I know this guy – let's call him Tom - he is now almost thirty-two years old and used to find himself in a place in life that was not really what he dreamed of. Tom was far away from functioning optimally and flourishing, showing robustness, generativity and growth. He was stuck. He has now made it out of this situation and leads a life he is very happy with. In my opinion, it is all because he was willing to share himself with other people. I'll give you some background.

Tom grew up with only his mother; he never got a chance to get to know his father, who left the country right after he was born. His mother had had a tough life herself and was not presented with many opportunities to build a career. She found work, but it was the kind that only pays for the bare minimum while requiring long hours of hard, manual labour. Tom was a very smart kid that needed to be properly challenged and stimulated in school and at home, but because of overcrowded classes and other failures in the educational system, that was not really an option for him. Thankfully, he had a huge passion for sports and invested hours and hours into training instead of hanging out in the streets. He trained so hard and performed so well that he even got a chance to go pro, but his mother couldn't afford the training camps and didn't want her son to be pursuing a career in sports in the first place.

Starting from the age of sixteen, Tom had to work while going to school and taking his classes to help his mother make a living. Education was not a priority. Avoiding financial ruin and surviving was much more important – even when exams were around the corner in his final year of high school. He couldn't afford to lose his job, which was an important source of family income, over studying, so he failed his final exams, and his high school diploma was never certified. He never gained the qualifications needed to go to university, and the family's financial situation didn't allow for him to invest time and money into taking on an apprenticeship. He found a few jobs in his hometown to keep him afloat, but he had to endure inhumane personal treatment and incredibly straining working hours.

I have known Tom for a couple of years now, and I was fortunate enough to witness his transformation. Tom went from someone who was unemployed with no degree, a lot of debt, unable to pay his rent every month or even put food on the table to a business owner, devoted husband and soon-to-be father.

An important enabler of his transformation was the woman who is now his wife, we'll call her Lisa. From what Tom told me, it was the first time in years that he had opened up to someone in the way that he did with Lisa, and she was a sort of emotional salvation for him. He let her see every part of himself, the good, the bad and the ugly, which certainly took a lot of courage seeing as most people he had met ignored the good after they witnessed the bad and the ugly. Lisa's complete acceptance of all his parts showed him that he was worthy of love, attention, care and affection – something he had really started doubting over the years. Tom always told me that he thought God's plan for him was to stay miserable and alone.

Anyway, Lisa had set herself up with a promising career. She was financially affluent and had a lot of contacts in the business world that she offered to hook Tom up with. At first, when Lisa offered that he could move in with her without having to contribute to the rent or lend him money so that he could afford the admission fee for a scholastic placement test for university, Tom declined. Over and over. He said that he relied on other people for help in the past, and they had screwed him over. He said that he had to handle his situation by himself.

After all, he had experienced thirty-two years of disappointments from people he thought had his best interest at heart, and he didn't want to make himself reliant on anyone.

Tom and I had a lot of conversations about his situation and the way he responded to Lisa's suggestions. To be honest, I really felt for her. Imagine how painful it is when the love you share with someone is apparently not enough for them to believe you'd never turn on them, even if you broke up. It must also be incredibly hurtful to see the person you love make such stubborn decisions, blocking their own development and not taking the opportunities available to them and needed to turn their life around, all because of pride, shame and fear. How heart-breaking it must have been for her to see someone she loved like that struggle so much when she could have easily helped him to achieve very much attainable solutions to improve his situation. Their relationship almost did not make it through his struggles. Tom continued to be miserable over the amounts of money he owed to people. He continued to be in agony over having to live in a crappy apartment and not being able to fulfil his dream of starting a family because he couldn't afford to raise children. Hell, he couldn't even afford the most basic requirements for his own life, like three balanced meals a day, even though he worked three jobs to pay his bills.

At some point, Lisa couldn't take it any longer. Not the fact that Tom was in a bad place, but the fact that he always had some excuse for why he wasn't able to get out of that bad place. He couldn't study and get a degree because his laptop was too old and slow. He couldn't sit down and read a book because his room was too dark and he had no comfortable chair. If he went to the library to read, he'd have to buy lunch somewhere close by to get through the day, which he couldn't afford. The list went on and on, all with petty reasons for why he couldn't put an end to his struggle. Lisa was about to break up with him and be done with the never-ending self-pity and self-victimisation. She felt like she was pouring her love and support into a bottomless pit, where it never helped produce any long-lasting positive effect.

Tom didn't want to lose her, of course, but he also saw no practicable way to improve and save his relationship. I pointed out to him that changing his situation of always struggling, never making it and never really being happy would mean giving up his identity of being a 'victim of his circumstances'. That's what his situation had grown to become over the years. That was now his identity, his emotional home. The victim is all he knew how to be. It was his mental model (to remind you of the previous chapter), his 'map of reality'[xvii]. He was the victim, and the world was cruel and untrustworthy. Apparently, that set off a series of realisations about his life that caused Tom to take on a new perspective of many things he had been pretty intransigent on until then. After weeks of reflection and hundreds of conversations with his girlfriend, Tom summarised his experience in the following words:

> *I understand now that the world around me continuously failed to show me appreciation and give me the feedback that I contribute value by being who I am or doing what I do. This produced a feeling that I would describe as estrangement or alienation from my environment and social contexts in general, which in turn inhibited my willingness to share myself, open up or disclose parts of myself. The fact that I had no meaningful relationship until I met my girlfriend and the fact that I still don't have purposeful work, robbed me of experiencing usefulness, purpose and belonging. But all that is going to change now.*

And indeed it did. For a long time, Tom's work and relationships didn't allow for him to experience self-actualisation, a life with a steady rhythm and a vitalised, coherent sense of self. He made plans with Lisa to move away and start over in a new city. He brought up the courage to rely on her for the next few years to pay the rent and provide for them until he could set himself up with a degree and a job. He proposed to her a year into their new life, and Lisa is now pregnant with their first child.

Tom's story is a great example of how closing ourselves off to others out of fear of becoming dependent on them or fear of giving them too much of our self – a weapon, then, they can use against us – limits us and holds us back. Doing this stands in the way of our growth and resilience, minimises goodness in our lives and limits generativity and creativity. If I could invite people to do one thing, it would be to let others offer them a helping hand, a listening ear or a truth-speaking mouth. We are all drawn to flee from what is uncomfortable; spending time and energy pushing away, reacting to and struggling with pain. Often, we do this in ways that add weight to what we're already carrying. Some of the things we go through are unavoidable – and appropriate. This sort of pain and struggle often reveals our emotional bandwidth and opens the door for introspection and getting to know ourselves better. It needs to be honoured with time and self-care. But it's also one-dimensional. Whatever the cause for the struggle or pain we endure, it presents us with the opportunity to reflect on our attachment to ideas, values, motives or people. Is there something destructive about this type of attachment? Are we holding on too tightly to something, rendering the attachment harmful? Obviously – if performed honestly and earnestly – this is a demanding inner conversation that we can have only with ourselves. We talked about this extensively in the previous chapter. But how are we supposed to reach those answers if the only perspective we have is our own? The human creative mind and its capability to solve problems is rooted in our species' unique ability to view objects, problems and the world in general through the eyes of others as a way to change our perspective.

If we're truly dedicated to seeking out the truth, perspective and, finally, progress in life, it means we also have to be willing to let our worldviews and our map of reality be challenged. The only way we can approach a degree of certainty about the validity of our reality maps is to expose it to the challenge and constructive criticism of other 'map makers'. The tendency to avoid challenge and resistance is basically inherent in human nature. But that doesn't mean it's beneficial or necessary, nor does it mean it's unchangeable behaviour. Openness and responsiveness to challenge are essential for progress and growth. Confrontation, resonance and challenges to our mental maps of reality and our worldview are the proverbial vegetables to our mental diet of junk food, as Mark Manson put it so nicely[xviii].

Just like vegetables, suffering is good for our bodies. It's biologically useful in a way because it's nature's way of inspiring change and progress. When we are dissatisfied and insecure to a certain degree, we put in the work to innovate, improve and thus survive. Our hardware is wired to make us experience dissatisfaction with what we have after a certain point and to make us expect we can be satisfied in attaining what we don't have. This inherent antagonism is what keeps us fighting and conquering and building and striving. Dissatisfaction, pain or suffering – in all its forms – is our mind's most effective way of igniting the fuse for taking action. Although physical pain is a feedback mechanism of our body to give us a sense of our own physical proportions, mental pain or challenge is doing the same in terms of our psychological proportions or mental bandwidth. It helps us understand our own limitations and spurs action to manage or overcome these limitations. However, resonance through sharing is not only a duty. It's also an inherent desire. Everyone and their grandmother are yearning for resonance; everyone wants a chance to tell their story and be heard. Social media has become an important arena hosting this fight for attention and resonance, forcing the whole world into the role of listeners to our stories. The constant posting and tweeting and gramming is nothing else but an – at times desperate – attempt to share and disclose ourselves to others. It's just easier to do so on social media than in real life because we can bias the presentation, thus controlling the kind of resonance and feedback we get. By doing this, we create echo chambers of pseudo-resonance, which, in truth, is just a quest for validation of the parts of our self we like, diverting attention away from the parts we fear might be challenged.

***

I'm sure many of you have had experiences where someone treated you unfairly or acted in a way that negatively affected you in some way, all so that so they could feel better about themselves. A recent example from my own experience actually had a significant impact on my career development and reputation in my company.

Every year in December, we receive a performance review at work. Based on this, people get raises or promotions. The performance review is a collection of feedback from peers, team members, superiors, clients and mentors. These individual pieces of feedback, especially the superiors' and the mentor's, are presented to us continuously throughout the year.

They serve as an indication of where we stand compared with our peers and how hard we still have to work to reach our goals. Of course, it's also a way to give us a chance to become aware of our potential for improvement and to work on achieving that before the end of year review.

My feedback throughout the year was good – on track to being promoted by the end of the year. I received a lot of praise from various superiors for my work. They also told me that I needed to work on my social skills here and there, basically to turn down the confidence a little and not risk bulldozing over my team members in front of clients or superiors. But all was good, everything was on track, and I was still a high potential in my peer group and, apparently ,invaluable for the company. Yet when the end-of-year performance review came, I was passed over for a promotion. My mentor, who is one of the most influential people in the company, told me that he really fought for my promotion, and the CEO and COO both wanted me to be promoted, but there was one person who didn't go along with the decision and blocked it completely. They made no secret about who blocked my promotion; the person's name and opinion is even stated in the performance review itself to explain the surprising outcome.

An important reason for why he didn't want to promote me was because, according to him, I am not a good team player. This was based on feedback he received from people on my team, especially the women. There were only four women on the team, so it wasn't hard for me to put two and two together and understand who must have complained about me. I asked her whether she'd be willing to sit down with me and talk everything through because even though I was told before that I should work on my coming across as too confident, the fact that my team members feel like I am terrible to work with was news to me.

She agreed to have a conversation. But it didn't go very well. A few days before I sat down with her, I found out that she had spread a lot of rumours about me in the firm. She warned new employees about me making everyone around here cry, and she told people that former colleagues had left because of me. She even went as far as to call the guy I was dating at the time to tell him he better break up with me because soon enough, he'd find out that I am a horrible person. I wasn't as shocked about the content of the rumours as I was disappointed about the idea that these conflicts had apparently been smouldering underneath a fake friend's surface for months and that no one ever confronted me about it. Going into our conversation with this new knowledge, I asked her why she would say things like that about me. What was her problem with me? Why didn't she confront me about her issues before blowing them up to the ridiculous importance they gained when the whole company started gossiping about me? Why did she feed false information to my superior, eventually making him block my promotion? (The fact that neither my mentor nor my superior talked to me to verify her claims is a yet another story.)

She was quite bitchy in her reply – I'm sorry but I have no alternative way to phrase her behaviour. She told me that I did in fact make her cry once, and if she was able to warn other colleagues about me, she would definitely do so. 'After all', she said, 'you know what you are like, and you shouldn't wonder why I did what I did'. But I did wonder. And I wanted her to tell me what the hell made her go to these lengths, affecting my career in such important ways. She told me that when she was first hired, she really liked me, and she was keen to work with me. But then, she realised that I 'make her feel stupid and incompetent' and that I was 'our boss' golden girl', leaving 'no space for her to shine'. She was convinced I did all this on purpose, 'playing dirty in the competition for recognition' and lacking consideration for her feelings. So she 'had to do what she had to do'.

Anyway, why do I bring this up now? You see, we don't usually make a conscious effort to question our motives for acting or wonder how our shadow on the inside would feel about the things we do in the outside world. We – or rather our rational conscious – don't bother ourselves with asking whether our shadow sympathises with our conscious plans and intentions. However, the contents of our conscious actions are undeniably influenced by our shadow's force, and we cannot become aware of and understand this unconscious, uncomfortable component of our reality map unless we share it. Yes, we need to share this part of ourselves, take the risk and expose it to challenge, but also empathy and maybe even unconditional love. Only then can we become fully aware of our self, shadows included, and we can consciously and purposefully develop strategies to monitor and manage our less-than-pleasant behaviours and attitudes. Of course, it's challenging for my colleague to disclose her thoughts and feelings about why she considers herself, quote, 'stupid and incompetent' compared with me. This, of course, shed a new light on her in the way she disclosed why she is so begrudged to see me advance and get credit. And of course, it's tough for me to hear that people feel bulldozed by me and that they perceive me as ignorant to their sensibilities. But neglecting – or even denying – these thoughts and feelings makes them a powerful instrument of evil. It is unbearable to think that we have to accept responsibility for all this 'guiltiness'. And that's why – if we don't accept and deal with our shadow-inherent evil, we start localising it in others.

What does this mean? It means we see our shadows in the people around us. We project. We shove everything we don't know and don't want to know about ourselves onto other people. In the example of me and my colleague, I was a very fitting screen for my colleague to project her insecurities on. And as the story also illustrates, nothing has a more alienating and wrecking effect on our relationships than the sanctimoniousness and moral complacency (on both our parts) that come from avoiding our mental maps being challenged. The mutual withdrawal of projections that we can achieve through constructively disclosing our self to others, on the other hand, is a powerful promoter of understanding and intimacy. Self-disclosure minimises self-justification and projection, helping us in mastering one of life's most challenging tasks: bearing the encounter with our self[xix].

**

So after everything we have talked about, how is it that we cultivate resilience to challenges through sharing? So far, we only discussed why sharing – or constructive self-disclosure – exposes us to challenge and constructive criticism of our worldview and why that helps us progress and grow. So we have the challenges part down, but what about the resilience part?

The thesaurus defines resilience as 'the power or ability to return to the original form, position, etc., after being bent, compressed, or stretched; elasticity'. So far so good. Applying the bending and stretching as a metaphor to human mentality, what we need to be able to return to our original form after having been bent, compressed or stretched (i.e., challenged) is knowing our way back. Knowing the way requires knowing ourselves. And sharing is one of the most important sources of that pivotal knowledge. When we practice constructive self-disclosure and gather feedback from others on our worldviews – our mental maps of reality – we *broaden* them. We broaden our worldviews, broaden our mindsets. And by doing that, we broaden our behavioural repertoires.

Let's talk about elasticity for a moment. Picture your life, your existence, as an elastic band or a string of pearls, or a tow or whatever you prefer. For most of our lives, we live out our existence in the middle of the string of human experience. Here, everything is normal and reassuring and regular. Challenges and failures pull on one end of our string and catapult our existence all the way over to the darkness-of-failure-and-disappointment-end of the spectrum. Success and achievements do the exact same thing. They'll pull on the other end of our string and will catapult us just as far away from our usual spot in the middle, shooting us over to the glare-of-recognition-and-praise end of the spectrum. Both places are equally blinding, and our psyche is completely incapable of untangling the connection between the way we experience great failure and the way we experience great success. The only thing that it is capable of feeling is the absolute value of this emotional equation. The exact distance that you have been flung away from yourself[xx].

So when we talk about resilience, what we mean is the ability to find our way back 'home' to the middle of our elastic band of human existence. And when we talk about truly knowing ourselves as being pivotal to finding our ways back to our origin after being bent, compressed and stretched and our elasticity has been tested, what we mean is knowing where our home is. It might be in your creativity, it might be in caring for your family, it might be in innovating, finding adventure, practising faith, providing service to others – it might be in growing tomatoes in your garden. To put it in the words of one of my favourite authors, Elisabeth Gilbert, the point is, we need to find our place where we can dedicate our energies with such singular devotion that the ultimate results become inconsequential[xxi]. It is some point on our mental map of reality to which we will always find the way because through challenge and constructive criticism, we have reached enough certainty about the validity of our reality maps to make sure we don't get lost. Resilience stems from a *coherent sense* of our self. We learn about ourselves through expressing ourselves, reflecting on our core self and engaging in creative learning through experiencing other humans' emotions. So dare to share! Sharing allows our existence to resonate; to reverberate. And through that we become more resilient. We amplify.

The Battle of Receiving or
Setting Meaningful Goals

On her fiftieth birthday, my mum hosted a big party with lots of friends and family. The people who were invited didn't all know each other, so at some point during the evening, after everyone already relaxed with a couple of drinks and appetizers, my mum gave a little speech to introduce everyone to everyone else. She started with her siblings and parents and then introduced us, her children. She introduced me with the following words (and I will never forget them because they were overly flattering and sweet compared with her usual way of expressing compliments): 'This is my brilliant daughter Rebecca. She has just finished her postgraduate degree this summer and is now working as a strategy consultant for the government. She just turned twenty-two. Isn't that amazing? I'm so proud of her. What she has achieved at such a young age shows an incredible amount of dedication and hard work – and most of all it is proof that she knows exactly what she wants'.

Is it all my mother's fault? Or in this case, is it all thanks to her? Whatever 'it' refers to, Sigmund Freud would have said yes. Well, modern-day psychoanalysts would say it's not all about the mothers, but looking at our caregivers to understand how our behaviours developed can shed light on a lot of things. Psychologists call it 'attachment theory'. Essentially, based on the kind of attention we received from our caregivers as children, we develop a behavioural system that guides us in our mental models and habits, especially concerning forming and maintaining relationships with our self and others. Attachment theory explores how our brains are programmed to help us survive and thrive in the environment we are born into. Children whose attachment to their caregivers is strong get most of their immediate needs met. They're probably well fed, frequently held, stimulatingly entertained and so on. Consequently, they can invest their time and energy in observing and interacting with their environment and thus better adapt to it.

The way in which we interact with our caregivers as children forms a behavioural continuum of emotion regulation and styles by which we become attached to our self and others later in life. The continuum ranges from attachment avoidance (characterised by overly organised strategies for controlling and minimising emotions) to attachment anxiety (characterised by uncontrolled, disorganised and ineffectively managed emotions). A secure attachment style falls in the middle of this continuum and is the base from which to reach out and gain experience in the world surrounding us.

The avoidant attachment style – resting on the first end of the spectrum – is likely to develop when children experience emotionally unavailable caregivers and insensitive, or even hostile, responses to their need for connection. Children are then likely to adapt to their situation by developing coping mechanisms of staying disconnected, first from their parents and later from virtually all other relationships. From a neuroscientific perspective, this is explained by the fact that the limbic system is basically starved without intimate nurture and does not receive the signals required for designing a repertoire of adequate social responses or emotional attunement. Later in life, children who have developed an avoidant attachment style are said to struggle with a lack of emotion and often cannot fully embody a participatory existence in social contexts. They may feel that they don't need human connection to survive or thrive and insist on maintaining their independence from others. When seriously challenged, people with an avoidant attachment style are likely to initiate an emotional shut down.

Moving towards the secure attachment style in the middle of the spectrum, we find children who experienced caregivers who were positively attuned to them and provided with a safe haven of consistent attention and affection. These children are likely to feel safe in exploring their environment and feel like they can trust others. They develop a resilient emotion regulation that includes healthy boundaries, individuation while still being capable of intimacy and social engagement. Later in life, children who have developed a secure attachment style will probably have greater confidence, more well-balanced relationships and the ability to both help other people get their needs met and receive the help needed to get their own needs met. Their relationships will probably be satisfying, and they will feel secure and connected to their partners without feeling the need to be together all the time. Their relationships are likely to feature honesty, independence and earnest connections.

Approaching the other far end of the spectrum, children who develop an ambivalent attachment style experienced inconsistent care and attention from their caregivers. Because of this inconsistency and the resulting doubt about whether their needs will be met, these children are likely to develop coping mechanisms by constantly looking out for cues and clues about what kind of responses their behaviours trigger in their caregivers. What is likely to result from this is an emotional back-

and-forth between needs being met and needs not being met. Hence, these children's understanding of the world is informed by 'I can want, but I cannot have'. So they keep wanting and are chronically dissatisfied. Later in life, children who developed an ambivalent attachment style may display a tendency to project these insecurities on new relationships and are unable to receive from others to get their needs met – simply because they aren't used to getting their needs met by receiving from others. Yet they are likely to feel desperate for love or affection and expect that their relationships must complete them or fix them. These people's emotional ambivalence manifests itself in behaviours such as being clingy, demanding, jealous or easily upset by small issues.

Finally, children who experienced a lot of mixed messages from their caregivers display a disorganised attachment style. Here, caregivers create situations for children that are insolvable and unwinnable, like asking their child to carry out a chore but then criticising them for how it's being done and maybe even going as far as punishing them for not having done what was asked of them. Children are likely to develop a pattern of not solving problems when exposed to these unwinnable situations and frightening, disorienting interactions with their caregivers over and over again. Resulting from the conflict between desiring the caregiver's closeness and wanting to detach from a frightening situation, children who have developed a disorganised attachment style are likely to display severe emotional conflicts later in life[xxii].

These templates we create in our early childhood to deal with our environment tell us how to respond to any situation later in life. But the world we live in as adults is obviously vastly different from the one we experienced when our attachment styles formed. So our response to life's events may now be unsuitable. Getting our needs met is at the essence of receiving. We all come out of our receiving histories and enter adult life displaying and prioritising different needs. Maybe what we need is protection. Or maybe what we need is space, freedom and adventure. These needs and the way in which we are able to receive them are rooted in the axioms we were raised by. These axioms set the tone for our caregivers' interactions with us. Were we raised with the axiom of autonomy or the axiom of loyalty? Were we raised to count on ourselves or taught that we can ask for help? Were we encouraged to state our needs or asked to intuit what other people want from us? Was someone taking care of our needs, or did we have to take care of our needs ourselves, making us a sort of 'parentified child'? What was our caregiver's axiom for boundaries? Were we soothed and held or beaten, our personal space invaded and violated?[xxiii] All these questions make up the voluminous and deeply rooted bottom of your iceberg (remember chapter three).

There is an intricate connection between our attachment styles and our confidence in ourselves and others. Ultimately, the axioms we are raised by and the attachment style we hence develop form our capability (or lack thereof) to receive and have our needs met later in life. How we receive care, attention, challenge, love, empathy, passion and so forth sets the tone for how we make choices and what goals we strive for to get our needs met. Our attachment style is also intimately connected to our motivational system. Our basic motivational system consists of both an approach system that steers activation or a certain appetite for results and an avoidance system that instead steers inhibition and aversion. When we evaluate certain environmental cues as indicating potential rewards for pursuing a goal, our approach system incites behaviour that drives us towards reaching this goal. It generates positive feelings, such as excitement, that make our brain anticipate the impending reward experience. On the other hand, when we evaluate environmental cues as indicating potential sacrifice involved in achieving a goal, our avoidance system energises behaviour that drives us away from these undesired outcomes. It generates negative feelings, such as anxiety, that prepare our brain for an impending harmful situation.

An anxious attachment style is related to a greater tendency for a motivational system of avoidance driven by the ever-present fear of making potential sacrifices for outcomes that aren't worthwhile. An avoidant attachment style is also related to a more profound motivation avoidance, but it is based on wanting to avoid any emotional investment when trying to attain a goal because of a fear to commit personal resources to unpredictable outcomes. In the same logic, avoidant attachment styles often result in individuals having less interest in and enjoyment of receiving social support. Avoidant attachment types strive to be self-reliant and in control. Anxious attachment types, on the other hand, strive for social approval, acceptance and being liked. So in short, what motivates us to achieve our goals and what gives our work meaning is very much connected to our attachment style and the way we are able to receive in order for our needs being met.

Precisely how these two systems are interconnected, though, remains unclear. Researchers consider it a possibility that the attachment system influences the development of the motivational system. Children with more secure attachment relationships, then, may tend to develop more active approach motivation systems because they have more frequent or consistent rewarding experiences. Children with attachment styles on the avoidance or anxiety end of the spectrum may tend to develop more active avoidance motivation systems because they have experienced unpredictability or aversion more frequently. However, it could also be possible that the attachment and motivational systems are partially overlapping and are influenced by shared genetic or neurological structures.

Now, what do we make of all this? Whatever the explanation for the correlation in attachment style and motivational style, the two systems are likely to be dynamically shaping each other throughout our lives. This is good because it means that by actively influencing one, we can drive change in the other.

By that I don't mean the kind of mental programming that is the stuff of most commercial life coaching. You know how life coaches always recommend to 'push through your pain and do what you dread anyway, just change your mindset or look at how other people are suffering even more than you have, so, surely, you, too, can do this? Well, that's not really a solution.

Those coaches are also the ones saying that when you're insecure, go stand in front of the mirror and compliment yourself until you yourself believe it. You're supposed to programme your mind by writing mantras on post-its and sticking them all around your apartment so that you read them all the time. You're supposed to get inspired by pursuing great ideas, to find your hunger never ending.

Blah. Blah. Blah.

To be honest, I'd call that some stupid shit – excuse my French. I don't think this fake-it-until-you-make-it approach really yields sustainable change. I want to talk about what we need to cultivate in terms of a 'mental culture', so to speak, that can actually help us successfully change the way we set goals, achieve goals and enable us to receive to get our needs met. In my opinion, the key is not to programme our mind to change *what* it does, but rather to become clear about *why* we want something.

I think that if someone is really successful at what he or she does, it's not because they're lucky. It's because they do something different than other people. And they work hard at sustaining that particular thing that sets them apart. This type of success leaves clues behind. By looking for the differences in successful people's behaviour, we can figure out what makes the difference in their results - and we can model that behavioural difference. In the fast-paced environments we find ourselves in, we live and die by our performance. We have to portray ourselves in the most professional manner, yet meritocracy isn't enough to set us apart from our peers. Complementing this professional manner with expressing a unique personality is what drives outstanding success. I am convinced that outstanding success is based on setting meaningful goals for yourself. When I think of some of the most outstanding and most successful people I know – people who show up every day to deliver excellence in their field – I think of people who are results oriented. They are team players. They execute strategy. They conquer adversity. They have a high-performing work ethic and are able to perform under pressure. They demonstrate disciplined time management. Elite dedication. Determination. Resilience. They're ambitious and inspirational, yet they remain coachable and are eager to learn. Demonstrating all of this every day requires much more than just skill and will power. If I were to study these people's habits and routines, I'm positive that what I'd find would come down to them having figured out *why* they have such passion for what they do. They do what they do because they have a *purpose*.

A purposeful life can come from many things. It can come from creating something with your work. It can come from enjoying beauty or even from demonstrating high moral behaviour in the face of hardship. One of my very impressive and successful friends says that her purpose is adding value. She wants to bring happiness, joy and laughter to a party. She wants to add a set of skills to a project. She wants to be able to offer help where help is needed. She wants to provide. She never works for getting something out of a situation, but rather for contributing something to a situation. She strives to continuously perfect her skills and abilities to achieve all that. She pushes through hard times, she endures setbacks, and she is tenacious about constructively dealing with criticism. She is aware that the kind of impact she wants to make will take time, so she sets meaningful long-term goals and cultivates patience for achieving them – all because she knows *why* she is putting in all this work. While she's at it, she sets high standards for herself. She wants to go deeper than average, do more than what is expected from her. She also knows that she needs to get her needs for appreciation and downtime met, so she expects respectful and direct communication and tends to herself to recharge her batteries.

Another one of my outstanding and successful friends finds her *why* in contributing to improvement in whatever she gets involved in – whether it is teaching someone a new skill or inspiring joy in other people. Her purpose is to understand almost every level or aspect of the things she works on. She wants to grasp the system of interdependencies that are at the heart of the many problems we're now trying to solve as societies. She wants to understand the system because she wants to achieve change on a meta-level that goes beyond the approaches other people have taken so far. To fulfil this purpose, my friend practices consistency and endurance, as well as patience and perseverance, even in times when she does not experience immediate success or goal achievement. This means that she sometimes does not immediately get her needs met, but she is able to delay gratification knowing that she will receive an abundance of meaningful accomplishments at a later point in time. Having set her meaningful goals is the absolute key to practising such endurance. Another aspect that is critical to her success is the earnest conviction that there is always something to learn from every single person and that one must have an open mind for new input.

For me, my purpose is growth. I want to be someone that others look at as a role model: I want to inspire growth in others and inspire them to aspire to greater heights. My purpose is to show up as my best self every day and demonstrate reflection, responsibility and commitment because it is my conviction that these traits make us flourish at the optimal level. What helps me unleash my *why* and define my purpose is the amount of time I spend introspecting and reflecting on myself. Because I do this, I know myself inside out. This caters to me knowing exactly what I want (in other words, being aware of my needs and knowing how to get them met) and having a lot of intrinsic motivation for sustainably achieving what I want. Because I know how to listen to – or rather interpret – my self and figure out what I want, I save lots of time on decision making. I don't go back and forth between options A and B for hours on end. I make choices swiftly, and I commit to them because I have no problem living with whatever consequences will be the result of my choice. I trust myself. I am established in my seat of self enough to not be shaken by criticism, resistance or failure. I am my own most shielded place of refuge, where I find peace, safety, solidity, understanding and patience. I take responsibility for everything I do or don't do. I don't want to go to bed at night thinking, 'I could have done more today' because I know that I'd be the only one to blame, the only one who is responsible for not achieving what I set out to.

You know what all three of us have in common besides having found our *why* and having set meaningful goals? It is something talked about in chapter three: getting our needs met is based on values that stretch beyond serving ourselves. We all work for values that are complex and challenging and transcend the immediate control over the world around us. I really think we're on to something here!

If you haven't found your why yet, study the lives of people who seem to have found their answers and compared them to those who haven't. Be around these people and model their behaviours. I am convinced that once we have figured out the *why* that gives meaning to our goals, we can figure out the *how* to go ahead and achieve those goals. Starting to think about *how* to achieve our goals immediately brings in the mind – a serious party pooper if you ask me. And it always brings fear as its plus one. Figuring out our purpose and understanding why we strive for what we strive for is the first step towards reaching clarity on the results we want to achieve[xxiv]. The mastery of our value iceberg that we talked about in chapter three is essential for this. But it is also essential to be completely honest with yourself, and to do this, we all need our shadow situation figured out first.

***

Coming back to Sigmund Freud, with whom we opened this chapter, I think we can refute one of his other famous statements: our primary drive in life is pleasure. I want to agree with Viktor Frankl instead, who maintained that our primary drive is actually the discovery and pursuit of what we personally find meaningful[xxv]. What drives humans is not the happy-go-lucky, tensionless state of pleasure, but rather the striving and – yes – the struggling for a worthwhile, meaningful purpose to be fulfilled.

Frankl was a prisoner in the Auschwitz concentration camp in World War II. During his time there, he studied the other inmates and what set the successful survivors apart from those who eventually fell victim to their imprisonment. The question that he was preoccupied with was, 'Does all this suffering, this dying around me, have a meaning?'. Frankl gathered that if that were not the case, if the suffering in the concentration camp had no meaning whatsoever, then ultimately, there would be no meaning to survival and freedom either. He maintained that the choice about how we respond to being challenged is the only thing that no one can ever take away from us. We are always have *something* as long as we have the freedom to find meaning in our hardship. We give meaning to our daily struggles, our everyday hustle, our unceasing grind by the way we respond to it. We can choose to find meaning in struggle and resistance and emerge from it with renewed purpose. In the spirit of Frankl's contemporary peer Fyodor Dostoyevsky, the only thing we should truly fear is being unworthy of our sufferings. As long as we have a *why*, we can always bear the *how*.

A little fun fact here: the Latin word *finis*, which is most commonly translated to 'end' or 'finish' has a second meaning. It also means 'a goal to reach'. As such, if we cannot see the end of our existence (i.e., if we don't experience challenges or hardship that feel like they could end our existence), we also cannot aim at an ultimate goal in life. We'd stop living and working for the future.

Consider this for a second: many of us have enough to live by, but nothing to live for.

We have means without meaning.

So first, we must set meaningful goals. Doing this goes beyond speaking in an affirmative way to ourselves and having a vision. Having meaningful goals is the key to embedding emotional attachment in our results and thus sparking a drive and motivation in us. Meaningful, compelling goals spur our growth and expansion through our successes. They also allow other areas of our lives to thrive when we are successful at achieving our goals. How do we set meaningful goals then? After having gone through a long process of introspection and reflection on our values and needs, we can turn our struggles into achievement, deriving an incentive to take action from life's inherently challenging struggles.

By cultivating a secure attachment style to our self and others, a style that allows us to freely explore – and at times encounter – challenge, we can apply better filters for what we meaningfully want to pursue and what truly matters, as well as what, on the other hand, doesn't matter. We can apply better filters for who matters, whose opinion matters and whose validation matters. By setting meaningful goals, we become able to connect to our values and our self in a way that allows us to detach from anything that prevents us from getting our needs met in a way that is obtainable and sustainable. Consequently, success, much like happiness, will ensue as an almost unintended side effect of our choice to commit to a cause that transcends our mere self or as the by-product of our choice to surrender to the meaning in the challenge and suffering we might be experiencing.

The Battle of Refusing or
Making Better Choices

In chapter two, we talked about how thoughtful and judicious withholding is just as much a part of relationships as pure and loyal noncontingent giving. In this chapter, we'll delve more into the withholding end of commitment and explore what it means to decidedly and responsibly calibrate where to draw boundaries.

Someone once told me that a good relationship comes down to two things: first, how well both people in the relationship accept their respective responsibilities and, second, the willingness of each person to reject the other and also accept being rejected by them. In other words, a healthy relationship is characterised by the presence of boundaries and the fact that each person takes responsibility for their own values and problems within those boundaries. I assume most people used to hand off this responsibility to their God or to religion in general. Now, many people replace the transcendent and spiritual with their relationships and seek almost divine perfection in them as well as in the person they're with. We assign godly attributes to our partners and kind of expect them to lift us from the mundane to the sublime through our relationship. Someone once called this 'an unholy muddle of two holy loves that can't help but disappoint'[xxvi]. We aspire to bring heaven down to earth, and somehow, now, happiness in life has transformed from an aspiration to a mandate, to something we feel entitled to being provided with through our relationships. We invest more into love and happiness than any generation before us, but all too often, our giving is transactional, and our asking stems from entitlement. In chapter two, we talked about this development and the contemporary consumer mentality of relationships. We touched upon how more often than not, we expect an ROI from our commitment or emotional investment. This leads to us waiting to meet the perfect person to complete us and fulfil us, instead of asking how we ourselves can take responsibility to grow and become the kind of person we expect to become through our partners.

We easily separate from our partners, not because we're per se unhappy, but because we fear or suspect we could be *happier*, ever indulging in the fear of missing out – on more immediate gratification and more endless variety, things we have come to consider a prerogative. This sense of entitlement and possessiveness is inherent to love (think jealousy, desire and longing), and at the same time, it's a distortion of the freedom and chosen surrender that is also so essential for its survival. We want to compel our partners to act in certain ways *for us*, to cater to *our* needs, to fulfil *our* every desire. Yet we don't want them to do it out of obligation, but rather because they *choose* to do so. And yet again, if they don't freely choose to do what we want them to do, we feel the disappointment of promise unfulfilled – they are supposed to love us. Do everything for us. So why aren't they?

Without the presence of clear boundaries and clearly assigned responsibility for certain problems and actions, we won't be able to connect to any strong values for ourselves, and we will lose sight of why we are doing what we do. Our only value or purpose becomes living up to a somewhat murky standard of a good relationship: making other people happy or being made happy by them. But we're not supposed to fix each other's problems to feel good about ourselves. Rather, each person in a relationship should take responsibility for their own problems so that they can then feel good about each other. In that sense, rejection is not a wall to permanently shield us off from others, but rather, it is a moving boundary that protects what is important to us while respecting what is important to others. In contrast to a wall that seems to be unquestionably right at any given time, a boundary is a changeable format that gives a frame to what is right in a given moment based on particular circumstances and priorities.

And just to clarify, this doesn't mean we can't support other people or be supported by them while taking responsibility for our self. Refusing a request doesn't mean we can't agree to finding an alternative solution. It simply means that the giving of such support should not be transactional and should not happen out of obligation. In the same way as the asking for such support should not happen out of entitlement. There ought to be a fluidity between relying on each other and having the confidence to leave each other without the fear of falling apart. You're anchored safely but have a long enough rode to be able to explore freely. We should be devoted, but we have to understand that we don't own each other.

Refusal can turn out to be the best way to support someone or be yourself supported in solving a problem sustainably. If you have a friend or partner who constantly complains to you about all the reasons why they can't get a job, it won't help them if you indulge in their self-pity. You can refuse to attend their pity party by simply telling them that you don't think you'd be a very good friend if you continued to listen to all the reasons why they'll never get a job. Instead, tell them you think they'd actually do better if they stopped finding excuses by talking to you and confirming their misery. Or for instance, imagine someone continuously complains to you about their boss and incompetent colleagues, but every time you suggest a strategy to solve the situation, they insist on a million reasons why that won't work or why you cannot possibly understand their incredibly complex plight well enough to offer a solution. Tell them that you don't think it would be a productive use of your time to keep talking about their issues. Step away from the negativity they're trapped in. Sure, it takes courage to set such clear limits. If everyone sets boundaries for themselves, the complexity and paradoxes of the interpersonal increase rather than diminish. However, it's most probably better for you and the person you're trying to help.

Often in relationships – especially romantic ones, but the same can apply to friendships or business partnerships – there are two roles: the pursuer and the pursued. One of them is more afraid to lose themselves, and one is more afraid to lose the other. The acceptance of these roles usually ends in a pattern of overblaming on the one hand and overaccepting blame on the other hand, all of which is driven by worry and anxiety. No one in this relationship will sustainably receive what they require to get their needs met.

Why do we bear witness to so many relationships in which one part of the couple seems to suck the life out of the other? I know couples in which one person ignores the other person's interests completely and, at times, even makes them feel bad about their interests. 'Why do you have to spend so much time with your family? You know I have a bad relationship with mine; do you have to rub it in my face all they time'? Or 'why do you spend so much time in your art studio? Art is a complete waste of time; I find nothing entertaining in it'. Another couple in my circle of friends has completely lost a sense of respectful communication with one another. Conversations first shifted from the personal to the virtual, and the text messages then became less frequent, more elusive and full of hurtful remarks. Often, this was followed by a period of 'love-bombing' to win each other back, just to then withdraw from each other again, which was followed by a period of 'rage-bombing' and incessant arguing or showing no more interest in one another – until the cycle starts again. Another couple I know constantly lives on ultimatums. Partner one, let's call her Mary, tries to hold the other, let's call him Thomas back because partner Thomas's personal growth makes Mary feel threatened and insecure. Mary creates a drama whenever Thomas chooses to do something that doesn't include her. Mary even went as far as to forbid Thomas from seeing a certain friend and participating in a certain activities, leaving Thomas to choose between his relationship and his personal life. The sad thing is, *having a choice* is not even obvious for Thomas. He still thinks he has something to lose or that he owes something to Mary. In yet another couple I know, one of the partners, I'll call him Evan, constantly keeps track of how many good things he has done for his partner, Ivy, and believes that his 'good deeds' are greater and worth more than what he is receiving from Ivy. Evan also keeps track Ivy's mistakes and uses them as ammunition in numerous senseless fights and arguments. Evan even goes as far as threatening to leave, saying 'who would want to be with you if you did xyz to them? You're lucky I'm willing to put up with you'.

Why do people go through this? Why don't they pack their things and leave? What could such a relationship possibly add to their lives and wellbeing? Where did they learn to behave like that? Who did they see do this? I can't help but wonder.

***

Do you remember back in the introduction when I talked about my enlightening flight back home from my business trip? I said I had reached the epitome of enlightenment on what it means to love, to be loved, to commit, to accept, to respect and to surrender. The podcast I listened to on the flight talked about how too many people in relationships demand their partners take responsibility for fixing them. They create more and more problems to get attention and be saved and fixed, all to feel worthy of love. Setting clear boundaries and taking responsibility for themselves doesn't excite them; it doesn't give them the 'emotional high' of feeling important. So an actual profession of love and care would be for the self-victimised person to say, 'You know what, this is my own bullshit, let me take some time for myself to fix it and just support me in doing so'. I was able to make progress and find peace with my ex's decision to end our relationship because I became able to untangle what his decision *did to me* from what his decision *meant to him*. And in that lay the beautiful unravelling that was triggered inside of me.

I realised that the reasons for which he ended our relationship were him taking responsibility for fixing his own problems. He was finally taking responsibility, refusing to ask me to save him any longer and refusing to hold me or our partnership accountable for solving his issues and for enabling his personal development. I realised that it was actually the ultimate profession of love and what we had was still an extraordinary basis for a great partnership. That realisation helped me a lot in accepting the breakup. He still blames his circumstances and other people for being in the bad situation he is in. He still doesn't really hold *himself* accountable for his problems. But he took a first step in the right direction by holding himself accountable for changing his circumstances. I felt really lucky that I am already (mostly) able to live by these paradigms, and I am convinced that it is at the core of my self-confidence and successes. I wanted him to be able to build himself up towards that as well. And for this, I had to respect his decision – even though I am equally convinced that such impasses are part and parcel of relationships and can – and should – be dealt with within the relationship framework. If we aim for the long haul, we should show resilience and stamina in the face of these challenges, award them patience and dedication and remain devoted to the togetherness. But that's another story, and we discussed it elsewhere in this book.

It's funny how in this beautiful unravelling I realised that giving, taking, asking, sharing and receiving all build the foundation for confidently refusing. And it's funny how it's the refusing part that completes genuine, long-lasting and earnest and sustainable love. When we make choices that go beyond what is comfortable and that involve refusing to take the easy way out (whether it's avoiding conflict with someone, avoiding making an effort for something or avoiding a demanding inner conversation with ourselves), we can see who is here for us unconditionally and who is by our side only when there are benefits to reap. Without that, no relationship really *means* anything. The choices we make don't really mean anything. Refusing something or saying no to something means making a choice, making a commitment. It means saying yes to what actually matters to us and is important to us. It means refusing alternatives to make more room and time for a few very meaningful and important things that truly matter to us. Refusing what is not in line with our values or what doesn't cater to meeting our or others' needs sustainably, allows us to focus intently on our meaningful goals. When we are established in our seat of self and accept responsibility for ourselves, we can be at peace with making these tough choices – even if it means cutting someone out of our lives or making other people unhappy. Respectfully refusing is liberating – and it's the result of the constant calibration of what we are and aren't responsible for in life.

There is a very enlightened quote by Joseph Conrad on this topic:

> *In order to move others deeply, we must deliberately allow ourselves to be carried away beyond the bounds of our normal sensibilities.*

What I think Joseph Conrad is trying to say is that cruelty and honesty are hard to separate at times. We may hurt other people's feelings by being blatantly honest with them and refusing something. Yet ultimately, our refusal may be for the better. We can't determine how people feel – and we are not responsible for their emotions (we talked about this in chapter two). By no means do I want to suggest that being able to refuse is rooted in a certain ruthlessness and carelessness for other peoples' thoughts and emotions. Rather, I think that being able to refuse is rooted in the idea that guilt is tolerable and that there is a sufficient establishment of self to bear it. Our potential guilt over not pleasing someone's every desire is tolerable. This in turn stems from the fact that we, too, accept responsibility for our own thoughts and feelings and let it be ok to be refused or rejected by others. It's up to us to deal with our feelings and problems. We shouldn't blame others for enticing our feelings, nor should we react to these enticed feelings in ways that restrict the 'enticer's' freedom. Let's not be manipulated into making sacrifices and being people pleasers because we are scared of feeling guilty, moving out of our comfort zone or taking responsibility.

Refusal does not only improve our individual wellbeing, but it also improves our relationships. Several studies have been conducted that explore the way choice influences partnerships[xxvii]. One of the most interesting ones is an experiment based on Robert Axelrod's prisoner's dilemma – a mind game that is well-known to most. The game studies the interaction between two players, or agents. The agents here are two people who are suspected of having committed a crime together. A detective puts them in separate rooms and interrogates both of them, hoping to get a confession out of at least one of them. Each of the suspected criminals can make one of two moves: cooperate or defect. In the case of cooperation, they deny any involvement of either suspect in the crime; in the case of defection, they admit to having committed the crime together.

The detective promises them rewards for their choices: if both players cooperate, they each get payoff C. If they both defect, they each get payoff D, which is lower than C. If one suspect defects and the other cooperates, the defector gets a payoff H, which is the highest out of all payoffs, and the co-operator gets a payoff L, which is the lowest out of all payoffs. For the sake of simplicity, lets imagine that C equals 3, D equals 1, H equals 5, and L equals 0. The payoff options for each agent are as follows:

If they both cooperate, each gets a payoff of three (3 | 3). If they both defect, they each get a payoff of one (1 | 1). If only one of them cooperates and the other defects, the co-operator gets a payoff of zero, and the defector gets a payoff of five (0 | 5). Without knowing what their partner in crime decided to do, the best move to make is to defect because it will guarantee a payoff: either the payoff will be one (1) if both defect or five

(5) if an agent is the only one defecting. However, if both agents decide to defect (i.e., going with the apparent best choice), they will each do worse than if they had both cooperated. And that, precisely, is the dilemma.

This game has been advanced in relationship studies. Here, agents play several rounds and use the game history between the agents to make choices about whether they accept or refuse a game partner. In other words, the agents are given the opportunity to assess the desirability of potential game partners and are able to refuse to play with those judged undesirable. In each new round, the agents update their expectations and assumptions about potential game partners based on past encounters.

The studies find that the introduction of this choice – of being able to refuse unacceptable game partners – fundamentally changes the way in which the agents interact and the characteristics that result in high payoffs. Having this choice allows the agents to increase their chances of collaborating with other cooperative agents. At the same time, refusal provides them with a way to protect themselves against defection while not having to defect themselves. Choice and refusal thus allow for lasting patterns of mutual cooperation to emerge. Likewise, parasites, or free riders, can infiltrate mutual cooperation. In these cases, the studies show that 'parasitic agents' are successful only as long as cooperative agents have an unlimited tolerance for parasitic behaviour. This means that parasitic agents are successful only until cooperative agents refuse to include them in the game.

What can we learn from this about refusal, rejecting and being rejected and making better choices? The iterated prisoner's dilemma's parasitic agent is a metaphor for anything toxic in our relationships and our lives in general. We can only profit from payoffs or good things in our day-to-day dilemmas when we have high enough thresholds for barring the toxic things and people from our lives and are able to refuse – and be refused. A lasting pattern of mutual cooperation, one that essentially describes a good relationship or partnership, emerges when two agents who demonstrate integrity accept responsibility and establish boundaries or thresholds against the undesirable things come together – which brings us back to the beginning of this chapter: a good relationship comes down to the presence of boundaries and the fact that each person takes responsibility for their own values and problems within those boundaries.

Why is it so important to many of us to please everyone to the point where we feel resentful and stressed because of it?

We're afraid to refuse because one of our biggest fears is being rejected. We're afraid that every time we refuse something, we will disappoint someone, make someone angry, hurt someone's feelings or appear unkind and rude. Having people think negatively of us is the ultimate rejection – whether we're told their negative thoughts about us or not doesn't even matter. The fear of rejection is enough to make us do everything in our power to avoid it. It's the thought that others look down on us and don't accept us that hurts the most. We worry that if we say no, we will feel humiliated, guilty or ashamed and will end up being alone, rejected or abandoned.

But refusing doesn't mean we're being rude, selfish or unkind. Again, where did we learn that? I suppose we learn as children to associate refusing a request with being bad mannered, ergo unkind, selfish and, ultimately, unlikeable. A lot of human behaviour is influenced by the desire to belong and be significant, so we work hard to avoid rejection. When our relational value to other people is in potential jeopardy, we begin acting in very obscure ways, as we saw in the examples earlier in this chapter about the many flawed, incomprehensible relationships around us.

That fact that we can accept losing our good graces with someone – whether justified or not, whether momentarily or permanently – at any given time is the ability to accept rejection. To know and accept our own limitations is the key to accepting other people's boundaries. As such, if we can accept being unsuccessful in pleasing someone – again, whether justified or not – we can accept that they have boundaries and may at times refuse to please us or be pleased by us. The reverse, that is, having our own boundaries and refusal abilities, is rooted in the same confidence. We should try to cultivate an awareness for the possibility of our relational value to others being low – and an acceptance for it because the relational value to our self is always high. Now is the time to cash in on the edifice built by learning to ask, give, take, share and receive in the ways we talked about in the previous chapters. Accept the possibility to be rejected and become comfortable with the idea that momentary rejection doesn't undermine commitment. Instead, it mandates a reciprocal active engagement and sense of resilience.

If we can cultivate this sense of accepting being rejected and daring to reject, we can begin to move more lightly despite our possibly very heavy burdens. Most importantly, we can relax and stop indulging in the constant fear of missing out. I used to practice 'FOMO' par excellence as a child; I'm not sure I remember being scolded more for anything by my mother. Her voice still rings in my ear twenty years later. Whenever we'd have dinner guests, I'd lurk around the living room, where all the adults were enjoying their aperitif. Not in the cute 'oh look at the host's cute daughter' way though. It was more in the 'why is she trying to get attention' kind of way. When my mother succeeded at finally sending me to bed, I'd come back downstairs at least three more times, telling her that I couldn't sleep – just to check on what everyone was up to. When my sisters had my mother's attention all to themselves, I'd be sure to barge into the room and demand to know (yes, I was that kind of kid) what they're talking about or what they're doing. Every time something like the dinner-party-lurking or the play-room-barge-in would happen, my mum would tell me that it's terrible how I am so afraid to miss out on something.

Now that I'm old(er) and wise(er), I observe this behaviour in other people around me, and I have to admit that my mum was totally right: it's incredibly annoying. So what if you're not liked by every single person? So what if you have travelled to less countries than other people? So what if your life seems less glamourous than those of the Instagram influencers do? The constant awareness of available alternatives to our current reality causes unfavourable comparisons, weakens commitment and prevents us from enjoying the present moment. We forget that the gold is buried in the depth of things, and we simply can't commit to digging deep into every single choice available to us. Only by refusing one thing can we make a meaningful choice for another that is actually worth having, a choice that is in line with our values and needs. That's how we can make better choices and go from optimising our time and energy to satisfying our needs. Refusing the default option, that is, stepping out of our default mode of 'fit in, please people' changes the meaning we assign to the choices we actually freely make.

The Battle of Imagining or
Tapping Into our Inner Resources

There is this woman I kind of worship. She's quite professional and rather disciplined. She had to overcome a few obstacles on her path, but now, she does pretty well for herself. Maybe you've heard of her? Her name is Beyoncé.

Of course she is *everything*. Super professional. Incredibly disciplined. Faced a million obstacles and now grosses millions. She has a verse in one of her songs that I pretty much made my life motto. She sings[xxviii]:

I dream it, I work hard, I grind 'til I own it.

And then, she also twirls on them haters, but that's not for now. 'I dream it, I work hard, I grind 'til I own it'. How do we get from imagining something or dreaming about something to generating the will power to grind until we own something? How do we tap into and make use of our inner resources?

I feel as though when people talk about their goals and how they didn't achieve them or only realised a part of them, they often give reasons such as 'I don't have the right contacts', 'I don't have enough capital', 'I don't have enough time' or 'I don't have the required knowledge'. In short, they are saying that they don't have sufficient or the appropriate resources. However, I think that what most people suffer from is not a resource-problem. Instead, it's a *resourcefulness*-problem. Most of us have strong intentions, but we end up not achieving our goals or achieving them in a quality that's different from what we set out to do. One way of overcoming that dissonance would be to simply set easier goals or lower our standards for what we consider successful. However, there must be a way to achieve the greatness we witness in others and to perform at our fullest potential, that is, really tap into our inner resources.

Having a core intention (I hope chapter three is coming to mind right now) is an important first step to really make use of our inner resources. Envisioning the ideal result that we want to come out of our core intention is another important step. Our imagination opens room for possibilities. It shows us in front of our inner eye what the world could look like if we acted a certain way or did a certain thing. In chapter four, we talked about creating this effect of opening up the realms of possibilities through sharing and resonating with others. Imagination is essentially the self resonating with the self, showing us the endless possibilities of who we could be or what we could achieve. Resonance, as we discussed earlier, is the source of growth, longevity, beauty, goodness, robustness, resilience, generativity and complexity – or in short: all the resources we need.

Our imaginative mind can work for us to uncover patterns within confusing or incomprehensible events and to find solutions that deal with this confusion and incomprehension. Our imagination is the space where parts of our experiences, the ones stemming from our personal past and reaching into the future, come together to make a whole. This room of wholeness is a space into which we can integrate our self and continuously reconstruct it. In this, the imaginative mind holds an incredible wealth of undeveloped material for a new understanding. And the beauty about the imaginative mind is that it is indifferent to evidence or truth. Freely roaming in the sanctuary of our imagination offers us possibilities for willpower creation that mere rational belief and perception can't supply.

One realm of the interpersonal where we tap into our imagination and basically throw rationality and perception overboard is, of course, love. Marcel Proust said it best when he claimed that it is not, in fact, our loved one who is responsible for our spring fever, but our own imagination[xxix]:

We need imagination, awakened by the uncertainty of being able to attain its object, to create a goal which hides

the other goal from us, and by substituting for sensual
pleasures the idea of penetrating another life, prevents us
from recognizing that pleasure, from tasting its true sa-
vour, from restricting it to its own range.

What we concoct in our imagination about our human objects of affection somehow unleashes incredible powers in us.
We are suddenly able to move heaven and earth to keep a loved
one by our side and make them happy. These powers find their
source simply in what we imagine could happen or unfold between a handsome stranger and us. When we love, we see
someone the way God (or whichever force you believe in)
might have intended them. These feelings, full of promise and
expectation, last as long as we entertain phantasies about that
person in our mind, and as long as we believe, there is still potential to realise them and bring them to life. I suppose this is
where outside observers see the blindness of love. But for the
people in love, this is their way of being omniscient – omniscient of all the possibility and limitless potential they imagine
in the other person. Of course, imagining a breakup or a big
fight between us and the object of our affection is just as important of a mental image as the phantasies of passion and fulfilment are. As we'll develop later on in this chapter, the imag-

inative mind is powerful enough to actually trigger physiological reactions to what our imagination comes up with. As such, by imagining the potential fallout of a relationship, we get a taste of what that devastation will feel like – and what we want to avoid at all costs.

Of course, as intelligent creatures, we are aware of the games our mind is playing. If we live and love in phantasies for too long without them actually translating into reality, we'll probably sooner or later stop to ask ourselves – what am I (still) doing here? I experienced this a lot in long-distance relationships when I wouldn't see my boyfriend for weeks and our relationship was basically living off memories and anticipations. I always wondered whether those were real feelings or whether they were just something artificial I talked myself into feeling. For the nerds among you, this is called metacognition. It's the uniquely human ability to think about our thoughts. We'll also take a closer look at such differences between beliefs and actions later on (the nerdy term for this is cognitive dissonance). For now, a different question comes to mind: Why not use the love-related force of the imaginative mind to unleash other kinds of resourceful inner powers and find the motivation we need to make our wildest dreams come true?

Sure, we don't have to accept Proust's and others' idea that love is entirely imagined. I, for one, am with Plato on this: love is a 'serious mental disease'. Jokes aside, emotions, after all, are the expression of our body's experience of responding to events or external cues. The physiological cues associated with emotions are relatively diffuse, however, leaving our experience open to our mind's interpretation of them based on previous situational cues and labels we assigned to them. In any case, if our emotions are an expression of our bodies experiencing the environment, this means we can change or transform our emotions by altering our physical actions, right?

The body and mind frequently get their signals crossed. An emotion produced by a physiological response to our environment can be confused for or can feed a second, unrelated emotion. Apparently, fear and lust share a lot of physiological cues, and our mind may respond with a racing heart, sweaty palms and heightened pulse while standing on a wobbly bridge 50 metres above a cliff, the same feeling of when we are intensely connected with and wanting another person. In the same way, events we merely imagine but may never have truly experienced can cause our physiology to change accordingly. This is what happens while watching horror movies, for example. Of course, we know that zombies and vampires aren't real, yet we fear them as we watch the movie. And yet again, even though we feel afraid, we don't usually jump out of our seat and run for our lives. Instead, we cling to our chair and squirm in cinematic enjoyment. However, what our imagination came up with resulted in a very real affective response. Its physiology matches that of real fear: the heart rate rises, the muscles clench and so on. Similar reactions are triggered when we imagine past events or possible future events. We may feel joy or invigoration as we think about a past blissful memory or feel devastation sweeping over us when we imagine our mother being in a horrible car accident tomorrow – even when she is sitting right across the table from us as we imagine her accident. So in summary, our imaginative states causally interact with our affective systems.

In an effort to regulate all this raging emotion, our brains are adamant about bridging any gaps between our internal and external circumstances – real or imagined. This process is called dissonance reduction and is a way to create as seamless a fit as possible between how we want to feel and what we actually experience. When there is a perceived inconsistency or dissonance between our beliefs and values on the one hand and our behaviours on the other hand, something must be adjusted to eliminate this discrepancy. Surprisingly – or maybe obviously – research finds that in most cases, we change our attitude to accommodate our behaviour rather than the other way around[xxx]. An example could be someone who buys an expensive car only to later discover that it is not comfortable on long drives. The dissonance here – very plainly – is between the person's belief that an expensive, high-quality car should be comfortable and their behaviour of having bought an uncomfortable car. Dissonance can be eliminated by reducing the importance of the dissonant belief: it doesn't matter whether the car is comfortable on long drives because it's mainly used for short trips anyway. Alternatively, dissonance can be reduced by adding more beliefs that are in line with the expressed behaviour: even though the car is not that comfortable, it's very safe, easy to handle and looks amazing – all qualities that expensive cars should have, too.

Another example could be when someone who considers themselves environmentally conscious and responsible takes flights – even to domestic destinations – several times a month. This person may change what they believe about flying: flying isn't actually that bad for the environment. Or they might change their beliefs on how to be an environmentally aware citizen: focusing on personal choices isn't the best way to protect the environment – only solving problems on a systemic level can bring about change. Or maybe the person will even give up considering themselves environmentally aware altogether.

These two example are pretty banal, but they reflect the stuff of day-to-day dissonance reduction. Most of this dissonance-reduction is usually insignificant, and our brain administers this kind of dissonance reduction without us even knowing it. We just move on. However, when important beliefs and actions conflict, we experience a greater level of psychological discomfort. There is no real way to measure the physiological reactions to reveal how each of us mentally construes aversive situations. But herein lies the central part of emotion generation: an interaction between physiological reactions and cognitive appraisals. They are complex but with a lot of potential to comprehend and influence performance and motivation.

To recap, dissonance reduction aims at reducing any gaps between behaviours and beliefs or between how we want to feel and what we actually experience. On an imaginative or mental plane, the internal way we want to feel can be understood either as a desire or as a belief. While belief aims to make one's imagined representation of experiences match the way the world actually is, desire operates the other way around, aiming to make the way the world actually is fit our mental representation of it. As such, the direction of adjustment is the main difference between the *conative* imagination that is desire and the *cognitive* imagination that is belief. Together, desire and belief – or the conative and cognitive imaginations – motivate action. Prime examples of how this can be turned into massive successes are Bill Gates and Steve Jobs, who both used their imaginations to envisage how computers could change the world, the way we work, how we educate our children, cure our sick and so on. High-level professional athletes also use their imagination and envision powers to unleash their full potential, tapping into the depths of their inner resources. An immensely vivid mental image can effectively prime their muscles to complete the exact same physical and technical action in a real competition. This visual rehearsal or imaginative training triggers neuro-transmitters to spark action in the muscles. A mental blueprint can thus be created, and the mind can be conditioned to anticipate reactions to certain pressures or problems that may arise. This facilitates or enhances future performance[xxxi].

But bearing in mind our discussion on dissonance reduction, the question comes to mind, whether Bill's and Steve's desires and beliefs are the reasons that causally explain their actions, giving them *normative reasons* to revolutionise the tech-industry? Or are their desires and beliefs reasons that justified and gave *good reasons* for their behaviour of, say, making important sacrifices to revolutionise the tech-industry?

I mentioned before that the main difference between belief and desire is the direction of dissonance reduction: beliefs aim to make our imagined representation of the world match the way the world really is and desires to the opposite by aiming to make the way the world actually is fit the way we imagine it to be. That means that action can't be motivated by belief only, because without desires we wouldn't be able to come up with ways to change the world according to the way it will fit our beliefs. Beliefs are empty without desires. In the same way, action can't be motivated by desire only, because without beliefs we wouldn't be able to see how we can satisfy our desires. Desires are blind without beliefs. In any case, I don't want to open an overly-philosophical discussion of the concepts used to explain human action. Whether we talk about intentions, purposes, goals, values, wants, desires, passions, or reasons (all of which have been discussed in this book) – they are interrelated factors that all have their rightful place in contemplating our personal motivation and paths to achievements, success and fulfilment.

Evidently, no amount of visualisation can replace actual training, just as imagining reaching a goal won't magically make it reality. But just as mental rehearsal can prime athletes for optimal performance, imagination can unleash the *resourcefulness* needed to motivate action to get the *resources* we seem to be lacking to reach our goals. We have to dream it, using our cognitive and conative imagination, and unlock our mind's creativity.[1] By doing this, we defeat habit with originality and can find solutions to almost any problem. But we also have to use our newly found motivation that has been spurred by beliefs and desires and work hard and 'grind 'til we own it'.

By now, we have established that the way we feel influences the way we behave, and we can transform the way we feel by transforming our physiology. I suppose that's why another trick athletes have up their sleeves is for them to assume the same posture on the court or on the field when they're down as they would when they're on top of their game. A certain tennis superstar revealed this as her secret to success. The point is that

---

[1] In my mother tongue, German, there is a more nuanced word to better describe what I mean: *Schöpfungskraft*

our core resource is our (emotional) state of mind. In our imagination, we find a way to unlock and unleash this resource and its powers in successful times and tough times alike. Sure, if someone has never succeeded at making their imagined accomplishments reality, it's hard to trust that as long as you're creative enough, caring enough and driven enough that you can make stuff happen. But even then, I am convinced that we each have something we're always successful at and that we can use as a starting point. Maybe it's always managing to make people laugh; maybe it's always being able to express compassion; or maybe it's always being able to enjoy and have fun. Whatever the case, this is where our creative potential[2] lies, waiting to be imagined into something great.

---

[2] German: *schöpferisches Potential*

Notes

---

[i] The ideas on the trinity are based on Clausewitz's work *Carl von Clausewitz, On War (Princeton University Press, 1976)* and informed by discussions *in Joanne C. Lo, Drawing Simplicity from Chaos, (The Strategy Bridge, August 2019)*

[ii] The podcast I am referring to is *The Tony Robbins Podcast.* The particular episode is *"Why do people cheat"*, part 1 and 2, in which Tony Robbins talks to couples therapist and researcher Esther Perel

[iii] This idea is inspired by Esther Perel, especially her book *Esther Perel, The State of Affairs (Harper, 2017)*

[iv] This idea is, again, inspired by the podcast mentioned above

[v] The concept of "shadow self" is put forward in *C.G. Jung, Archetypes and the collective Unconscious*. For a more profound understanding, I also read *C.G. Jung, The Undiscovered Self: The Dilemma of the Individual in Modern Society (Berkley; Reissue edition, 2006)* and connected ideas from both work in my chapter.

[vi] This idea is inspired by Michael A. Singer. One of his well-known books, for example, is *Michael A. Singer, The Untethered Soul (New Harbinger Publications/ Noetic Books, 2007)*

[vii] This is a concept from Zen Buddhism that was first introduced by Zen master Eihei Dogen (1200-1253)

[viii] Researcher and life coach Tony Robbins often touches on this in his podcast.

[ix] The ideas discussed in this paragraph are inspired by M Scott Peck, who develops some of the points mentioned here in his book *M Scott Peck, The Road Less Travelled (Touchstone; Anniversary edition, 2003)*

[x] Maria Miceli and Cristiano Castelfranchia studied this relationship in their research. Their paper *Maria Miceli, Cristiano Castelfranchia, Reconsidering the Differences between Shame and Guilt (European Journal of Psychology, 2018)* is especially intriguing.

[xi] The term "parasitism" is also used in this context by M Scot Peck in his book *M Scott Peck, The Road Less Travelled (Touchstone; Anniversary edition, 2003)*

[xii] Researcher and life coach Tony Robbins first claimed the "six basic human needs" and they are an important concept he uses in many aspects of his work.

[xiii] In his speech *Oration on the dignity of the human being (Oratio de hominis dignitate)* from 1486, the humanist Pico della Mirandola contemplates the idea that human nature is a repository of instruments by which each individual can shape their life. He suggests that the core of human dignity is precisely this freedom of choice and the responsibilities attached to it.

[xiv] See for example *Barbara L. Frederickson, The broaden-and-build theory of positive emotions (Philosophical transactions of the Royal Society of London. Series B, Biological sciences, 2004)*, which I first read for sociology class at university and revisited in the process of writing this book.

[xv] The concept of the "extended mind" was introduced in the 1998 research of Andy Clark and David Chalmers.

[xvi] The concept of "switching" and it being essential for identity formation was developed by Harrison White in *Harrison White, Identity and Control (Princeton University Press, 1992)* as well as *Harrison White, Interfaces (REVUE - Magazine for the Next Society, 2012)*. I studied White extensively while writing my Masters thesis at university.

[xvii] M Scott Peck uses the metaphor of "mental map of reality" in his book *M Scott Peck, The Road Less Travelled (Touchstone; Anniversary edition, 2003)*.

[xviii] In his book *Mark Manson, The Subtle Art of Not Giving a F*ck (Harper; International ed. Edition, 2016)*

[xix] The ideas discussed in this paragraph are inspired by *C.G. Jung, The Undiscovered Self: The Dilemma of the Individual in Modern Society (Berkley; Reissue edition, 2006)*.

[xx] In her 2014 Ted *Talk "Success, failure and the drive to keep creating"*, Elisabeth Gilbert uses this simile.

[xxi] This is also from Elisabeth Gilbert's 2014 Ted Talk *"Success, failure and the drive to keep creating"*.

[xxii] The ideas on attachment theory discussed in this chapter are informed by various articles and studies: *Zipora Shechtman and Judith Rybko, Attachment Style and Observed Initial Self-Disclosure as Explanatory Variables of Group Functioning (Group Dynamics: Theory, Research, and Practice, 2004)*; *Kenneth D. Locke, Attachment styles and interpersonal approach and avoidance goals in everyday couple interactions (Personal Relationships, 2008)*; *Courtney Ackerman, What is*

Attachment Theory? Bowlby's 4 Stages Explained (Positive Psychology Studies, 2018)

[xxiii] The ideas of "axioms we were raised by" are inspired by Esther Perel.

[xxiv] The ideas discussed in this paragraph are inspired by Tony Robbins.

[xxv] Frankl summarised and published his research in *Viktor Frankl, Man's Search for Meaning (Rider; Export e. edition, 2008)*.

[xxvi] This is attributed to Robert Johnson, an analyst of C.G. Jung's school of psychology, who claims in *Robert Johnson, We: the Psychology of Romantic Love (HarperOne; Reprint edition, 2009)* that in our largely secular society, romantic love has become "the single greatest energy system in the Western psyche. In our culture it has supplanted religion as the arena in which men and women seek meaning, transcendence, wholeness and ecstasy". The notion is also picked up and discussed by Esther Perel in her book *Esther Perel, The State of Affairs (Harper, 2017)*.

[xxvii] I used the extensive literature review and research results in *E. Ann Stanley, Dan Ashlock and Mark D. Smucker, Iterated prisoner's dilemma with choice and refusal of partners: Evolutionary results (European Conference on Artificial Life, 1995)* to inform the ideas put forward in my book.

[xxviii] This verse is from Beyoncé's song *Formation (2016)*.

[xxix] This idea is hidden in Proust's novel *Marcel Proust, In Search of Lost Time: In the Shadow of Young Girls in Flower*

(Penguin Classics; 2 edition, 2003) that explores themes of love and the bloom of youth.

xxx See for example the research presented in *Sebastian Cancino-Montecinos, Fredrik Björklund and Torun Lindholm, Dissonance reduction as emotion regulation: Attitude change is related to positive emotions in the induced compliance paradigm (PLoS One, 2018).*

xxxi The ideas in this paragraph have been informed by various papers: *Kate F. Hays, The Psychology of Performance in Sport and Other Domains in The Oxford Handbook of Sport and Performance Psychology (Oxford University Press, 2012); Lydia Ievleva and Peter C. Terry, Applying Sport Psychology to Business (British Psychological Society, 2008)*; as well as my personal conversations with a professional athlete.

Lightning Source UK Ltd.
Milton Keynes UK
UKHW011955171019
351815UK00002B/76/P